COSMIC FORCES OF MU
⤙ VOLUME ONE ⤚

COLONEL JAMES CHURCHWARD

COSMIC FORCES OF MU

VOLUME ONE

BY
COL. JAMES CHURCHWARD

ILLUSTRATED

BE, BOOKS
CW DANIEL

COSMIC FORCES OF MU, Volume 1

BE, Books / The C. W. Daniel Company Ltd. Co-publication
©1934 James Churchward
Published by the Author, Mount Vernon, New York
Warner Books/Paperback Library, New York, 1968
Neville Spearman Ltd., London, 1970

Printed 1992, reprinted 1993, 1998 by
BE, Books c/o Brotherhood of Life, Inc.
110 Dartmouth SE, Albuquerque, New Mexico 87106, U.S.A.
http://www.brotherhoodoflife.com
ISBN 0-914732-27-7 (U.S.A.)
&
The C. W. Daniel Company Ltd., 1 Church Path
Saffron Walden, ESSEX CB10 1JP, England
ISBN 0-85207-243-0 (U.K.)

Cover art: *Cosmic Forces of Mu* ©1991, Jeffrey K. Bedrick

This work is affectionately dedicated to my wife
Louise H. Churchward
who during many years helped and encouraged
me to bring this my best work to fruition.

J. C.

The first edition of COSMIC FORCES *consists of
2000 copies, the first 500 of which are bound
semi-de-luxe, with cloth back and paper sides.
No further printing of these semi-de-luxe copies
will be made. They are numbered from 1 to 500.*

This is copy number 423.

Acknowledgments

I HAVE now to thank the late Dr. W. J. Holland, Director of the Carnegie Museum, Pittsburg, Pa., for his kindly advice and suggestions about the order of compiling the material contained in this work. His recommendations I have found most helpful.

To my friend Dr. C. W. Gilmore, Curator of Vertebrates of the National Museum, Washington, D. C., I have to give special thanks on behalf of myself and readers for his great kindness and magnificent work in making restorations of ancient life to illustrate one of the chapters of this work. The restorations were made from actual fossils in the museum. They are now of world-wide renown among scientists and are considered the best restorations ever modelled of these past forms of animal life.

Contents

List of Illustrations

Introduction

DURING the teachings of early man, science was a part of religion. They were considered and looked upon as twin sisters. The first teachings of man were that there was an almighty, all-powerful, Creative God and that man owed his existence to Him.

Then followed the teachings that man was a special creation, possessing a something that no other form of Creation on earth possessed—a soul or spirit. He was taught that this soul had everlasting life and never died. The material body returned to earth from whence it came, this released the soul, and it continued on. Apparently, when the foregoing was thoroughly instilled into his mind and he thoroughly comprehended it, lessons in science followed. Teachings were given that showed him the laws and works of Creation, such as the infinite wisdom in the arrangement of the universe, the perfectly natural laws governing all creations and the perfect manner in which they are being carried out, etc., etc.

With the knowledge of these sciences, man was enabled to apprehend more fully the power, the wisdom and the Great Divine Love of the Creator.

These scientific teachings brought man in closer touch, and gave him a better understanding and oneness with his Heavenly Father.

All of these original sciences which were taught man were in a form so simple that man, in his then uncultured state, could thoroughly understand them. Understanding them gave him implicit faith in and love for his Creator.

These simple sciences were taught without theorising, and not a semblance of theology or technology was used. Plain, simple facts were taught, and explained only. Yet these sciences today are called the Cosmic Sciences. They are called Cosmic because, simple as they were to the ancients, they are not understood and are beyond the knowledge of present man. The question may be asked, why? The answer to which is: Because the ancient scientific garden has been choked up with the rank weeds of theory, technology, theology, misconceptions, inventions, capped with childish dreams which have neither rhyme or reason, and all of which are toally at variance with the natural laws which govern throughout the universe.

The deplorable state of the present time has been brought about generally by two factors:

First. The egotism of present man, and his inordinate craving for publicity, wishing to be thought the topmost pinnacle of the Mountain of Science—absolutely forgetting or ignoring the fact that there is only one Great One.

The greatest height man can ever attain is the great honor of being one of His selected agents for conveying the knowledge of truth. Man is only the agent; the greatness belongs to Him alone: but great is the man who is the agent, because he has received an honor beyond all earthly honors that could be bestowed upon him.

Second. Man's turning from the worship of God to the worship of mammon, though while worshipping mammon he professes the worship of God. He deceives himself only; he does not deceive the Almighty. The ultimate object of acquiring vast material interests is to enslave fellow man. These material-worshipping, rooting hogs may wish to call it by another name, but slavery is the name, no other. And while this goes on, peace cannot rest upon this earth.

In the garden of nature will be found the great school for learning true science, for nature is the school-house for the higher learning, where man is taught to prepare himself for his undying future.

To help man in these studies, information was given him in the form of writings called:

The Sacred and Inspired Writings

which explained religion and science.

Where are those writings now? Are they lost? No, not lost but scattered, and the reading of them forgotten, but, according to the Divine Laws, the scattered parts will be brought together again and re-learnt. Then the myths which have permeated science for thousands of years will disappear like mists in the rays of a bright sun.

The contents of this volume are the translations of a few scraps of the Sacred Inspired Writings—Scientific Section—which have fallen to my lot to discover and record. The translations are poor, I admit, but they are the best I can do with my limited knowledge.

I say that no one can translate the ancient writings giving every minute detail as written, read and understood by the ancients. Anyone who says he can has no respect for the truth. The utmost anyone can do is to give the general meaning. This I feel confident I have done.

There are many reasons why minute details of the ancient writings cannot be given by modern translators; for instance, a symbol or hieroglyph forms a radical and the radical has many meanings, like the modern oriental words—mootoo, erekathu, etc. The actual meaning of the word depends on how it is pronounced and accentuated. There is nothing in the ancient glyph or in the spelling of the modern words which I have quoted to intimate which meaning is intended.

[15]

With the modern we learn from hearing and teaching. In the ancient we cannot hear or be taught; therefore no one at the present time can make translations of the ancient in a manner to give every minor detail as perfect, full and comprehensive as the ancients themselves understood it.

Fifteen thousand years ago these writings were perfectly understood by our forefathers. In Egypt I find that they were fairly maintained down to the time of Moses. Moses understood them. Ezra, who compiled the Old Testament, did not. (800 B.C.)

Two thousand years ago they were understood in about five monasteries. How well they are understood in these monasteries today I do not know. Much has been forgotten. A very prominent scientist after reading this MS. remarked, "I hope it will be a long time before this is published, because it will send all of our professors and teachers back into the student class. Such an upheaval as this would cause would be most lamentable."

Are truths lamentable?

Chapter I. Origin of the Great Forces

Before attempting to show the origin of forces, I will define what a force is.

A force is that which makes changes in the position of bodies, and sometimes changes in the body itself. No body or matter, however infinitesimally small or ponderously large, can make any change without the aid of a force.

All forces known as atomic forces are only secondary forces governed by some superior force. The superior force moves the atoms and the atoms produce or convey another or secondary force—the superior force is the responsible one. There is one great infinite force that governs all.

A force may be obvious to the sense of feeling, but no force is obvious to the sense of vision.

Forces cannot be stored in superheated bodies, neither can an exhausted force be regenerated in cold areas.

Forces are positive and negative. For every positive force there is a negative one.

Certain of the great forces are limitless in their scope and power, reaching from one celestial body to another. Forces are responsible for the movements of all bodies throughout the universe.

Forces have their affinities, repellents and neutrals in other forces.

Some of the *earthly* forces have affinities, repellents and neutrals in elements.

Two forces meeting, may do one of two things: They may form a neutral zone where both become non-effective. Example, "When an irresistible force meets an immovable object"—a neutral zone is formed and the struggle ends.

When one force is stronger than the other, it conquers it and passes on.

The movements of forces are vibratory. A live coal may be placed in the palm of the hand without burning it, provided the owner of the hand raises his inner vibrations (higher force) above the vibrations of the heat force.

A neutral zone is formed between the burning coal and the flesh of the hand, beyond which the heat force cannot pass.

There is one supreme infinite force which has created four great primary forces. Through and from these four great forces all other forces are generated, and are therefore secondary. These four great forces are governing the physical universe today, and are working under the command or will of the One Supreme Infinite Force.

This supreme force is the power which started and keeps all other forces working throughout the universe.

This supreme force is incomprehensible to man. Being incomprehensible He can neither be pictured or named. He is The Nameless.

It is without doubt appreciated by everyone that we are surrounded and living in the midst of forces whose power is inconceivable: and yet, while we are in their midst and they are moving and governing the immense celestial bodies, we do not feel them; they do not touch us; and if not told by observation of their effects, we should be unaware of their presence and existence. Why is it that these appalling forces do not in any way affect us? First, because being elementary, we are neutral to them, and, second, they are ultra to our minds and bodies.

Man is so created and constituted that everything connected

[18]

with him has range. His ear can only receive sounds that are within a given range, just so high and no higher, just so low and no lower; beyond these points he cannot hear the sounds, although they may exist, because they are out of his range of reception.

I am about to explain the origin of the great forces, but to successfully build up either a structure or a theory a solid foundation is necessary. I will start my foundation by illustrating the movements of the celestial bodies with a set of cogwheels.

It will be seen that there is a central or primary force, illustrated by a triangle within a circle and having a dot in the

The universe as a set of cogwheels

center. This circle has no cogs, but is starting the first wheels with cogs into movement. These cogs represent secondary forces, generated by the movements of atoms, or conveyed through the atoms. The first cogwheel meshes into the second with its secondary forces and starts it, and this one the next, and so on to the uttermost ends of the universe.

As an example let us take our solar system.

A superior sun is meshing in her cogs or forces with our suns, cogs or forces. Being more powerful, this superior sun is revolving our sun, and thereby producing secondary forces. Our sun's forces thus produced are meshing in with the forces of her satellites and revolving those which are not dead. Thus our solar system is a miniature example of the workings of the whole universe.

All governing bodies from the first sun down to the last must revolve on their axis; and, to enable them to do so every revolving body must have a hard crust and soft center; for without this combination they cannot revolve and generate forces.

A solid body without a soft center is a dead body,—it can neither revolve on its axis or generate forces. Our moon and the planet Mercury are examples of dead bodies.

All movements of bodies after leaving the first cogwheel body down to the little moons swinging around the planets are worked and controlled by secondary forces, emanating from the first great supreme primary force.

The central power is not governed by any force, for it is the origin and governor of all forces. If it were governed by some other force it would not be the center, there would be something beyond it. The central power is the Great Infinite Force which has always existed and will continue on forever.

The foregoing is my foundation.

THE SCIENCES OF THE FIRST CIVILIZATION. At the time of the destruction of Mu—the Motherland—which occurred about 10,000 B.C. the sciences which were then known and practised were the development of over 100,000 years of study and experience, if we date their commencement from a stated time.

Today we are practising sciences, such as they are, that have been developed within the past 500 years. We are probably now treading the same road which our forefathers trod over 100,000 years ago. That they experienced as many troubles and failures then as now, there can be no question of doubt: for legends by the score tell us that this was so. The symbolical legend about the Tower of Babel is one of them.

Scientific human nature has ever been the same—very egotistical, jealous, domineering, selfish, craving for prominence, desiring fame, regardless of whether it is deserved or not, with a most profound worship of Mammon. All of which are quagmires and quicksands in the paths of science; and all those who walk this road are doomed to disappear and be forgotten directly they are gone. They have done nothing for themselves or for mankind.

In India I found many clay tablets brought there from the Motherland by the Naacals. They originally brought a library of over 10,000 tablets; thus it will be seen that what I found formed only a single paragraph in a long story. All except a very few of these Naacal tablets were on the creation, and the workings of the Cosmic Forces.

Upon their disclosures I commenced to write this book. Details about the finding of these tablets were given in my first book, "The Lost Continent of Mu."

Sixty years ago I was sitting in the shade of feathery palms in India, with my old preceptor, the Rishi, deciphering and translating these precious Naacal relics. Today I find myself alone, in America, sitting at a library table deciphering other sets of ancient writings, over 3000 in one set alone.

This set consists of stone tablets found by William Niven in Mexico, at spots varying from 4 to 6 miles north and northwest of Mexico City. William Niven has generously and kindly copied and photographed them all, and sent to me the copies for deciphering if I can.

From some of these tablets it is shown that they are more than 12,000 years old, but how much older I cannot say.

All but a few of them are picture writings, and are tableaus depicting sentences from the Sacred Inspired Writings of Mu. A great number are about the Creation, and over 1000 about the Cosmic Forces, giving their origin and workings, also showing what life is, and how elements are given life.

I find in these American tablets many links missing in the Oriental Naacal tablets. As both sets, the American and the Oriental, came originally from the same source—the Sacred Inspired Writings, we can make a start in an inquiry into the mysteries of nature, and learn how our great scientific forefathers saw it after more than a hundred thousand years of study and experience.

I have made numerous experiments, following the Naacal writings. One experiment extended, continuously, day and night, for a period of seven years. This experiment was made for the purpose of satisfying myself as to the cause of the various changes in the forms of life which have taken place since the advent of life on earth.

The result of this experiment is given in Chapter V, page 135, "Evolution Impossible."

At this point it will no doubt interest some of my readers to see the form of these ancient American tablets, with their symbols and pictorial form of writing. Also how they are

deciphered and read. These are pictures which fate has pre-
served and handed to us for study, that we may correct the
scientific errors into which we have fallen.

I will first take a few of Niven's Mexican tablets, then follow them with a few from the American Mound Builders
virtually coming out of our own front gardens.

Tablet No. 1231. The key to universal movements

This is probably the most valuable tablet in the whole of
Niven's Mexican collection of over 3000; as it clears up two
important points in ancient man's cosmogony, and explains
what has hitherto been looked upon as mythical.

As will be seen, when understood, there is nothing mythical about it, but something very profound, and beyond our knowledge of today.

This tablet tells a tale that is far-reaching. It first tells us that there are four great primary forces, which were used in Creation, and are now governing the movements of all bodies throughout the universe. It tells us that these forces are working from west to east, and carry all celestial bodies in the direction of west to east and further it shows that all living revolving bodies revolve on their axes from west to east.

It tells us that these forces by their actions cause the revolving bodies to continue their force, so that apparently the force comes from the movements of the body. The scientific world calls this atomic force. There is no such a thing as an atomic force. What is now called an atomic force by scientists does not obtain its energy from elements of the atom. The atomic element is simply a collector, carrier and distributor of the portions of primary forces that have been handed to it.

Revolving bodies, like the earth, may be termed in popular language, transformers; receiving from the primary forces portions of the main volume, which each body distributes throughout itself, according to nature's requirements.

Coming through the atom, which is kept constantly charged, scientists have assumed that it is the atom which creates the force, which is erroneous, for the atom is only a conveyor.

We hear a lot about smashing the atom to get its forces. Why smash a brook of running water and scatter it? Why not turn the water into account as it flows on? By smashing the brook a run of water with its power is cut off. By smashing the atom the flow of forces through it is destroyed. The ancients used the flow, they did not destroy it.

Returning to the tablet. It shows the origin of forces

and the power that turns the first cogwheel in our diagram on page 19.

It clearly and distinctly shows and states that: The Power is the Will and Command of the Infinite.

My readers may ask: How are these deductions arrived at? I will anticipate this question by dissecting and translating the vignette on the tablet.

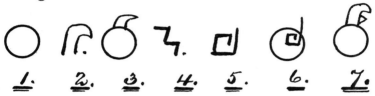

1. The central circle symbolizes the Creator—the Infinite.

2. The curved arms symbolize the four primary forces.

3. The arms project from the circle. Being joined to the circle, they are coming from it. That is, these forces emanate from the Creator.

4. Within each arm is written its name. The glyph here used is equivalent to architect and geometrician, so that it says these are the four great architects, the four great geometricians, the four great builders.

5. Within the circle is the Hieratic letter H, the alphabetical symbol of the great four. Being within the circle designates that they are in the Creator, and as one of the names in an arm is connected with the Hieratic letter H it designates that the four are to be called the four great geometricians, etc.

Being within the circle, it is within the Creator. Being within and coming from the Creator, it becomes His will and command; thus showing that the actual origin of all forces is the Creator.

[25]

6. Here is shown the Hieratic letter H within the circle, the alphabetical symbol of the great four.

7. Each of the arms, a great primary force, has projecting from it an arrowhead, the Motherland's symbol of activity, thus showing that these forces did not cease their work on the completion of creation but are continuing on in some capacity.

The ancients thoroughly understood this, for in this vignette they depict it and in their writings they say: "When the sacred ones had completed creation, they were given charge of the physical universe."

This is not appreciated today, nor will it be until after it is learnt what life really is, how it is created and afterwards maintained. At present the world is far from this knowledge, otherwise the bizarre theory of evolution could not be considered.

MEXICAN TABLET NO. 1086. A CONVENTIONAL BIRD. I am using this tablet to confirm the previous one, inasmuch as I claim that the primary forces originate directly from the Creator.

In all parts of the earth, among all ancient peoples, birds were one of the symbols for the creative forces. In America it was and is called the "Thunder Bird." In the "Lost Continent of Mu" Indian legends and their beliefs about the "Thunder Bird" are given. I will now confirm Tablet No. 1086 regarding the origin of forces.

The eye of this bird is a double, which was the Uighur symbol for the Deity or Creator.

The Hieratic letter H—the alphabetical symbol for the four great primary forces—the sacred four. This is shown projecting from the body, therefore projecting or coming out of the Creator Himself. Beneath the letter H is an apron

[26]

composed of four bars. Four was the numeral symbol for the sacred four.

Mexican Tablet No. 1086

TRUNCATED FIGURES. In this group there are 116 tablets, and with no two identically alike. (Nos. 494, 1623, 1138 and 513, page 28.)

They are purely conventional figures, and were not intended to represent any form of life. As a matter of fact they are completely made up of symbols and the old form of numeral writing.

They are designed to show the origin and workings of two of the four great primary forces.

THE BODIES. Their bodies are either in the form of a crysalis or a pod, used as a symbol for the home of forces, but referring to two only of the primary four.

[27]

No. 494

No. 1623

No. 1138

No. 513

Mexican truncated figures

BODY LINES. The bodies of these various figures have lines and symbols engraved upon them. The lines are the old temple esoteric form of writing and explain what particular action of the forces the figure is symbolizing. The numeral writing carries a hidden meaning. The numbers used in this form of writing are from 1 to 10, inclusive.

Numeral writing was the temple writing in Egypt down to 500 B.C and probably a little later. We know this from the Greek, Pythagoras, who when in Egypt was initiated into the Sacred Mysteries. When he returned to Greece he taught his pupils "to honor God with numbers." On every one of these 116 tablets the Creator is mentioned as the One from which the great primary forces originate.

THE ELEPHANT TRUNK. The trunk is a symbol telling us which way or direction the forces move throughout the universe.

All movements are from west to east and circular or elliptical.

All the heavenly bodies are moving from west to east.

All revolving bodies revolve from west to east.

One particular force controls these movements either directly or indirectly.

Every one of these figures is facing west with their trunks curling towards the east, symbolizing the circular movement of the forces.

Some have a second trunk at the back like tablets Nos. 494 and 513. This trunk is curled within the head and still travelling from west to east. This trunk symbolizes the gyroscopical force, which possibly is the daughter of the great centripetal force,—the force which collected the gases, compacted them and formed worlds out of them. This great centripetal force, as soon as the body revolved, became dead

[29]

as far as that world was concerned; then the gyroscopical force took up its parents' work and keeps its world upright.

THEIR LIMBS. Their limbs number from none (see tablet No. 1138), to four as shown in tablet No. 1623.

These mark the movements of the sun.

For two reasons I have taken many of the pictures which are found in America as examples to show the accuracy of the Oriental pictures and writings on the Cosmic Forces:

First. Because when other countries are being shown to have had super-civilizations, America at the time was not behind them.

Second. To show that our scientists can find more at home here in America that is worth while, than by gallivanting all over the world searching for the remains of very early man. Some ambitious ones declare that it is to be the very first man with them or nothing. If this is actually what they want they would be more likely to find him here in America than in the Gobi Desert or some other out-of-the-way corner of Asia.

Egypt, India, Greece and all ancient histories tell us that man's advent on earth was on Mu—an ancient continent that now forms the bed of the Pacific Ocean.

It is from written Oriental records, with their explanatory vignettes, that I have attempted to give some insight into the ancient Cosmic Forces of the earth's first great civilization, the foundation of all true sciences.

In the writings of this great civilization we are told that the universe is governed and controlled by four great primary forces, that these great forces originate and emanate from the Creator, that "they are his executors in carrying out His commands, His desires, His wishes."

The ancients, understanding the origin of these forces, and the power that has always worked them, so revered them that they could never find a name sufficiently divine to call them. Their attempts to give them more appropriate names led to their being known by many. I have collected a list of over 50.

The ancient scientists, apparently, on all occasions made drawings descriptive of the working of them. Following I am showing some of them, also giving their meanings:

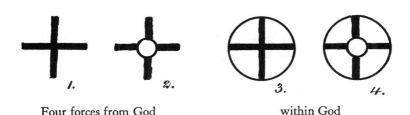

1. 2. 3. 4.

Four forces from God   within God

Fig. 1. This is the original symbol used for speaking of the four great forces. I first found it in the Sacred Writings of Mu, which were written over 70,000 years ago. It is prominent in Mexican writings and tablets, also among the American Mound Builders' remains.

Fig. 2. The same four forces, showing that they emanate from the Deity as the Creator. This is also found in Mexico, the Mound Builders and the Cliff Dwellers of North America.

Fig. 3. Another form of expressing the same conception as Fig 2. It is not as old as the previous figures but was universal throughout the world, and especially prominent among the Mound Builders' remains.

Fig. 4. A contemporary symbol with Fig. 3. It simply emphasizes the fact that the four great forces originate in the Creator. It was very universally used and is very prominent in the Mexican tablets and the Mound Builders' remains.

[31]

Rays proceeding from the four forces

An American Mound Builders of America symbol telling us that the rays of the sun emanate from the workings of the "forces within him," and that these forces come out of the four great primary forces.

These are two other Mound Builders' symbols, showing the molten center of a living revolving body grinding against the hard crust of the body, thus producing a frictional line between the two. This line regenerates exhausted forces and returns them to the hard crust, there to await nature's call for other work. Details of this work are found in the Sacred Writings. The Egyptian scribe Aua, 1200 B.C., wrote considerably concerning this phenomenon.

LEFT: Earth's molten center moving west to east. RIGHT: Sun's molten center revolving west to east

Mound Dwellers   Mexican
The four forces working from west to east

This is a Mound Builders' symbol, which has identically the same meaning as the Mexican Tablet No. 1231, on page 23. The only difference between the two is that the Mexican has a written explanation on it.

They both say that there are four great forces that emanate from the Deity, and that they travel from west to east around a center.

This is also a Mound Builders' symbol. In all of my research work I have only come across one other like it. That

[32]

Mound dwellers light and dark. Rays and forces

was on a very old Hindu document dating about 3000 B.C. It symbolizes the sun emitting both light and dark rays, and says that both the light and the dark rays are carriers of forces, and that they are all moving from west to east in a curve.

This symbol says that the rays with their forces form a curve as they shoot through space, so that a ray coming from our sun would not strike the earth in a direct line but on a curve. Whether this is true I cannot say. It is up to those who know more about the Heavens than I do to say.

Forces returning to their mother base

Another Mound Builders' symbol illustrating the workings of the earthly forces and also showing that they originally come from the Creator.

Around the hard crust of the earth are shown a number of scallops. They begin and end at the outer crust of the earth. This endless symbol, for it is shown joined to the hard crust, designated among the ancients completion; whatever it represents is shown to have completed its work. The central cross in the figure is its caption; therefore that which is referred to is the forces.

The complete reading says the earth's forces leave her body and pass into the atmosphere; after performing their several duties there, they become exhausted; when exhausted they return to the great frictional line there to be regenerated, then passed out into the storehouse—the hard crust—there to await the next call from nature. The earth's forces cannot pass out beyond the earth's atmosphere into space, because there is nothing in space that can hold them.

The sun's pole oscillates.
Mound builders

The Mound Builders are here telling us that the sun's poles oscillate, which means that He is being controlled by a Superior Sun; therefore, as it is revolving and being controlled, our sun is a cool body having a soft center with a hard crust.

I think these examples are all sufficient to show that America at one time, and not so very long ago, enjoyed a civilization second to none on earth—at least, as far as the knowledge of the workings of the Cosmic Forces are concerned, which is the true science upon which the universe has been built.

Chapter II. The Earth's Forces

Various phenomena which are constantly coming before our eyes show us that the earth is generating forces.

Nature has never been prodigal in her works, so that these forces are being generated for works which are being carried on by nature. It will be my endeavor to show what these forces are, how they are generated, and, to some extent, show the works they are carrying on. To do this, I shall have to start from the very beginning of the earth, when she was nothing but a whirling mass of gases, a nebula, to enable me to see how the earth's forces were commenced and afterwards completed. This is necessary to show the polar forces and the very important part they play in the movements of the earth.

Before the formation of a crust to the earth, no earthly centrifugal force existed, nor could there be until after the centripetal force, which had been working the gases to a center, surrendered the matter. As there was no regular revolving movement of the mass to generate a centrifugal force, there could be no gyroscopical force.

The gases forming the earth, and down to the time of a molten crust, were rolled and tumbled around in every conceivable manner by the centripetal force which was forming her. This was necessary to mold her into spherical form. This rough handling had to be, otherwise the earth would have assumed some irregular form.

As soon as a crust was formed, the earth was a sphere having a hard outside crust and a molten and gaseous center—

or soft. And when she ceased cooling, the condition was the same, with the exception that the crust was thickened.

The next point to consider is: of what use is this soft center? It must be of some use, otherwise it would never have been retained within the crust of the earth.

The earth and the universe are our great schoolhouse to lead us to a higher learning. There are many, many lessons which nature would teach us, but they remain unlearned. Nature has taught us that everything that exists is in a temporary form only, and that nothing can really die or be lost. All must, in some form or other, continue on forever. Everything that exists, and every condition that is brought about, is for some special purpose and for the accomplishment of something for some special object.

As the earth has a hard crust and a soft center, it is a condition. Being a condition, it has been brought about to result in some special service. Now comes the question: what is the special function or service that is being performed on account of this condition?

On the equator, on its surface, the solid hard crust of the earth is traveling at a rate of speed of about 1500 feet per second. The earth's central molten matter is traveling in the same direction, but much slower than the hard crust. Between the two substances—the one going faster than the other—a frictional line is produced.

When the earth commenced to revolve on her axis, she commenced to generate three great forces:

A great primary force

A centrifugal force, and

A gyroscopical force.

The early volcanic workings during the Archaean time show that the great centripetal force quickly surrendered its control of the earth to the newly born earthly forces. This change was accomplished before the newly formed crust had time to become cold and brittle. This is demonstrated by the waves and flexures in the Gneiss rocks, which I have in my geological work called the secondary rocks, as they were laid down upon the granite which I have called the primary rock. These volcanic workings took place before the waters rested on the face of the earth.

The earth's centrifugal force may be put into two parts or divisions,—the first division, within the crust of the earth, and the second division, from the earth's surface out.

With the advent of the earth's centrifugal force came the birth of the earth's gyroscopical force.

As soon as the gyroscopical force came into existence, it began to settle the earth in an upright position, which afterwards became permanent. When the waters and the atmosphere were formed, the centripetal force relinquished all claims on the government of the earth's movements.

The earth was then taken full charge of by the sun's great magnetic forces in conjunction with the earth's forces. The combination of these forces ever afterwards governed all of the movements of the earth.

During the time the original shell or crust of the earth was cooling, the inner division of the centrifugal force which was turned into the gyroscopical force after striking the earth's solid crust should have had a tendency to cup or flatten the polar regions. It would do so if the forces worked then as now, because when these forces first began their work, the crust was very soft, plastic, and pliable, and capable of being molded. We find that the forces did work then as now, because the ends of the earth, the polar regions, are flattened. The flattening of the ends of the earth could not have been accomplished had the crust of the earth, then, at the commencement of the working of the forces, been cold, hard, and brittle. It is thus shown that the earth commenced to revolve on her axis directly after the first initial crust was formed, and before it became cold and unyielding.

Up to the time of the formation of the waters and the atmosphere, the cooling and solidifying was slow, but after the waters and atmosphere were formed, the cooling and solidifying became more rapid. At first the earth's crust, the storage-plant of her forces, was very thin and incapable of holding all of the primary force which she was developing. As it thickened, however, the storage-plant for her forces was increased. As soon as the waters and atmosphere were formed, vast volumes of the primary force were drawn out into the atmosphere by the sun's affinitive forces. Volumes were drawn out until the holding capacity of the atmosphere was filled. Then the actual thickening of the earth's crust commenced, for it was practically impossible to cool deeper until some of the primary force was withdrawn. The heat force forms a large percentage of the earth's primary force.

As the earth's crust thickened and greater volumes of the primary force were held in her body, the resistance to the sun's pull increased. Consequently the velocity of the earth's revolutions was proportionately increased.

The thickening of the earth's crust went on until a neutral zone was struck. Then it could cool and solidify no deeper. At this point the earth had attained her highest velocity, which she has maintained down to the present time.

I have heretofore said that a soft center was retained within the crust of the earth for some special purpose and for some definite function. That purpose was to provide a frictional line where the earth's forces could be generated and regenerated. This phenomenon is explained in the article below, entitled "The Primary Force."

Following natural laws, the earth's central centrifugal force combined with the gyroscopical force should carry up and pack the molten matter against the end, and with it volumes of the primary force that had not yet been placed in the storehouse.

At the top end the molten matter should assume the form of a cup, with a flattened end on the surface of the crust on the outside. A natural result would be a great aggregation of the primary force within the cup, resulting in the supermagnetizing of the flattened end on the outside. This area should be more highly magnetized than any other area on the earth's surface. We find it is so, therefore this phenomenon is a fact and is proven by the magnetic compass being drawn towards the pole from all parts of the earth, and ceasing to be drawn when within the magnetic cup. By this I mean the needle ceases to act after it passes the edge of the cup. I have been told by explorers who have been within the cup that the needle tries to stand on its end. The molten cup is formed at the pole because the forces carry the matter upwards with a circular movement. An encased centrifugal force turns to a gyroscopical force and carries matter upwards and at the top cups it. The earth's molten matter is encased. An ordinary example of an encased centrifugal force is stirring a cup of liquid with a spoon rapidly. The liquid at the top assumes the form of a cup.

THE PRIMARY FORCE. The primary being the principal one of the earth's forces, I shall consider it first.

This force is generated and regenerated by the grinding of the molten matter in the earth's center against her harder outside crust. It is the friction along the line of contact between the molten matter and the crust that forms the magnet which attracts and draws back exhausted forces for regeneration. It is this magnet which holds regenerated forces in their storehouse against the pull of the sun's affinitive forces, and it is this magnet that draws all elementary matter towards itself, popularly called the force of gravity.

Forces are like elements, in that they have always existed and will continue to exist forever. They cannot die or pass away, and, like elements, after performing a work they become exhausted; the element returns to mother earth, the force returns to the frictional line for regeneration; thus they both return to their respective places of generation for regeneration.

The frictional line of contact forms a most powerful dual magnet. One part controls the forces of the electro-magnetic division of the primary force. The other part of the magnet controls all elementary matter. Hereafter I shall refer to the frictional line as the central magnet.

As before stated, what is termed our solar heat is an earthly force which is drawn by affinitive rays of the sun from the earth's body out into the atmosphere.

After many trials and experiments, I have succeeded in photographing the movements of the atmosphere caused by the forces passing through it as they leave the body of the earth.

This photograph is not of the forces or of the atmosphere. Neither the forces nor the atmosphere can be photographed. It is of shadows cast on a suitable background.

From this picture it is shown that the earth's forces leave her body in the form of dark invisible flames. These flames divide up and disperse in streams and flashings too indistinct to show in the picture. Some of these dark flames or columns

The earth's primary force leaving her body passing out into the atmosphere

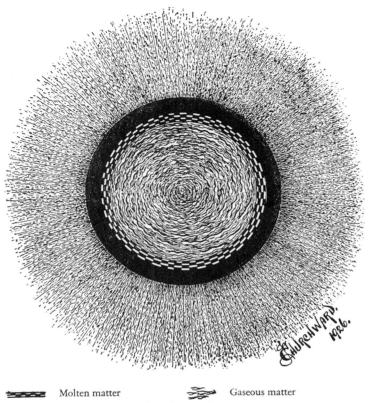

─────── Molten matter   ⟿ Gaseous matter

The primary force

attain a considerable height, several feet. When the volume of these flames increases, as it does during certain hours of the day, the length of the flame increases, and with it rapidity of movements of the whole group.

Most of the earthly forces are specialized in that they cannot leave the earth and her atmosphere and pass out into space, there to become lost. Therefore these earthly forces cannot be drawn out beyond the atmosphere.

Certain of the sun's rays carry forces that are affinitive to the forces of the earth's electro-magnetic division. These sun's forces fall upon the earth's surface with his rays. They attract and draw from the surface of the earth's body certain of the earthly forces out into the atmosphere. While the sun's forces are drawing and pulling on the earth's forces which are in her body, the great central magnet is endeavoring and trying to keep them in the earth's hard crust. This point should be specially noted because I shall hereafter show that it is one of the factors in revolving the earth on her axis.

One great fact must be fully appreciated; that is: when the earth's forces are drawn from her body out into the atmosphere, they can be drawn no further, and there they must remain until claimed by the central magnet. Another very important point ever to remember is: The earth's atmosphere has a limit to its holding capacity; it can only hold and carry in suspension just so much and no more. Any surplus over its holding capacity becomes an extreme and gets spilled. This is very plainly shown us in everyday atmospheric phenomena. As an example: When the sun's affinitive forces succeed in drawing from the earth's body a greater volume of the forces than the atmosphere can carry, the surpluses accumulate, join, aggregate, and return to their storehouse, the earth's hard crust, being thus drawn back by the central dual magnet. Lightning is the example. Lightning is an accumulation of the overcharge in the atmosphere of the electro-magnetic division of the earth's primary force, in the act of either returning to the earth or equalizing in the atmosphere.

Another very important point to be constantly kept in mind is: The earth's hard crust is the storehouse of her forces; and that the earth's primary force permeates the whole crust of the earth and her atmosphere and everything on the face of the earth.

Oxygen plays a most important point in the earth's makeup. It is a many-sided element and under certain circumstances has a dual polarity. In the scientific teachings of today great stress is laid on polarity; in many cases this is unquestionably the wrong word to use, as it is misleading. First of all, let us see what polarity as named by scientists is. Polarity is the working of one force against another, and the phenomenon of polarity results under the great law governing neutral zones. As an example, scientists call the earth a negative pole! Why? On account of its repellent or centrifugal force which is working outwards all the time. This, however, is only comparative, otherwise all loose matter on the surface of the earth would be hurled out beyond the atmosphere into space. This does not happen because the earth's central magnet is the positive and stronger force. There is a neutral zone between the two. The zone depends on the elements in question, for with some elements this neutral zone does not exist. As an example, throw a stone into the air at a given point; it stops its upward flight and is drawn back again by the magnet or positive force. Oxygen has as many sides as Joseph's coat had colors. It is one of the great affinities of many of the branches of the electro-magnetic division—primary force—and is especially affinitive to the Vital or Life-Force, a branch of the electro-magnetic division. It has been the great hardener in forming the earth's solid crust, for no crystal can be formed without it. The whole earth is made up of oxides. Ogygen is contained in all rocks, soils, metals, water, and the atmosphere. In this material we find the storage-plant of the primary force.

Oxygen in combination with other elements is the conductor of the primary force to the outer limit of her atmosphere.

What do we actually know about chemistry today? Nothing! What we know can be written on the first page of a 2000-leaved volume, the balance would be filled up by what we do not know, and all because we have failed to learn the connection between the elements and the forces.

I shall hereafter show under the head lines of the sun's forces that magnetic forces are coming from the sun to the earth which are extremely affinitive to all forces of the electromagnetic division of the earth's primary force. The sun's forces being so much more powerful than the earth's magnet enables the sun to draw from the body of the earth her forces even against the magnetic power of the central magnet and elementary attractions, to the extent of what the atmosphere can carry in suspension.

When two or more forces are working against each other, neutral zones are formed. A neutral zone is where the two forces equalize in strength. If there were no neutral zones, the whole universe would be chaotic in its movements; the celestial bodies would have no definite routes and would be constantly colliding and running into each other. All system throughout the universe would be eliminated.

A neutral zone is a line or point where two forces which are working in opposition to each other become equalized in strength. Generally, when two forces emanate from the same source, in fact, I might say always, one of the two forces starts much stronger than the other, but weakens faster as it proceeds from the point of generation. At a given point or line,

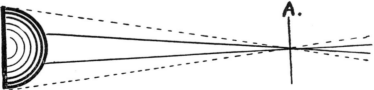

Neutral zone. At the point "A" the two forces equalize

the weaker one becomes equal to the stronger one, so that from this passing point as they continue on, the stronger becomes the weaker as shown in the illustration on page 46.

In this cut I shall suppose the dotted line to be a magnetic force a, a, and the straight lines a centrifugal force b, b. At N. Z. they become equal in power, hence at this point there is a neutral zone. Below I give two examples which may be tested out by anyone. They are simplicity itself.

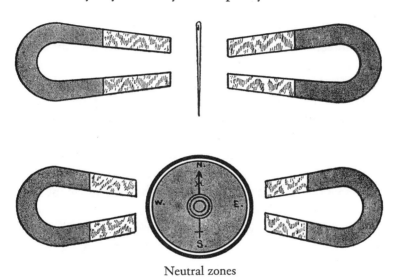

Neutral zones

Place an ordinary sewing needle in the exact center between two equally powerful magnets. The needle is in no way affected because it is in a neutral zone. To prove that it is in a neutral zone, take away one of the magnets. The needle immediately jumps to the remaining magnet and attaches itself to it.

Instead of using a sewing needle, take a magnetic compass. This experiment is much more delicate. While the compass

[47]

is midway between the two magnets, the needle will point north. Remove one of the magnets, and the point of the needle will immediately swing around and point to the remaining magnet. While the two magnets were present, the needle was in a neutral zone. The magnetic forces were working on both sides of the compass, but their powers were equalized.

THE ELECTRO-MAGNETIC. I have termed this division of the earth's primary force the electro-magnetic division because it contains the compound force electricity, the compound life or vital force, the heat force, the light force, various magnetic forces, and other innumerable forces which I have been unable to isolate.

The forces of this division originate and carry on life, and, in combination with certain forces from the sun and two secondary earthly forces control all movements of the earth.

All forces in this division are exceedingly affinitive to certain of the sun's forces. The sun's forces give them life and movement. Without the sun's forces they are dormant. The sun's forces are absolutely neutral to all earthly elements. Elements are in no way affected by any of the sun's forces. The sun's forces affect the earth's forces only. All apparent affectations of earthly elements by the sun are the works of earthly forces set into action by affinitive forces from the sun.

The earth's central magnet is antagonistic to the sun's forces: for, while the sun's affinitive forces are drawing the earthly forces from the earth's body out into the atmosphere, the central magnet is using all of its power to prevent it and to keep the earth's forces within her body. Were this not so, the earth could not be revolved on her axis.

As before stated, there are apparently hundreds of distinctive forces that go to make up the electro-magnetic division.

Rays of all colors, shades, and tints are in combination with the various forces, and each force is carried in its own particular colored ray. All rays carry a force regardless of whether they are light and visible or whether they are ultra, dark, and invisible. As a matter of fact, less than one-tenth of the rays carrying forces are invisible to the human eye. They are extremes, and although every one of them has a color, the color is indistinguishable because it is an extreme color. Each and every one of the forces is used by nature, in some special manner, for some special purpose.

I shall hereafter show how the visible light rays which carry the light force can be separated and isolated from the dark rays which carry the heat and magnetic forces. There are two dark rays which carry the heat and magnetic forces which can be conjointly isolated. But I have been unable to isolate the heat ray from the magnetic so as to isolate the heat alone. In all of my attempts to do so, and they have not been few, the magnetic has invariably crept in. If the magnetic ray could be repelled from the heat, then the heat would stand alone—isolated.

I shall now give a diagram showing a partial division of the electro-magnetic, starting from the central frictional line.

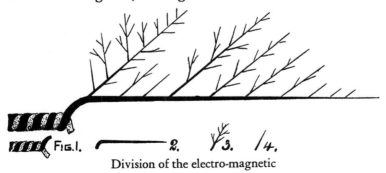

Division of the electro-magnetic

Fig. 1. Represents the earth's full primary force at the central frictional line. As will be seen, the forces are shown intertwined by diagonal lines like a rope. The black rings represent the electro-magnetic and the light rings the cold magnetic forces.

Fig. 2. The horizontal black heavy line represents the full volume of the electro-magnetic as it passes from the earth's body out into the atmosphere. In the earth's very specialized atmosphere, the various forces are filtered out from the main stream, so that each force becomes qualified to perform the duty assigned to it by nature. The forces filter out in two forms, single and compound. Probably some of the compounds filter into singles afterwards.

Fig. 3. Shows the forces leaving the main stream as compounds.

Fig. 4. Shows a single force filtering out from the main stream.

There are innumerable functions performed by the electro-magnetic division, and a volume might be written on each one, so that to go into details about all would fill a library. I shall simply dwell on a few. A chapter will be devoted to each —all that is possible in this curtailed work. I am simply blazing a path for others to continue.

Judging by old records, the study of the mystic forces appears to have been the principal theme of the ancients of the earth's first great civilization 50,000 to 100,000 years ago, and which they appear to have fairly mastered.

The subject of forces with us, today, is an unploughed field. Not a sod has been turned over by our present civilization.

When the first great civilization was wiped out, mankind went down hill as regards learning. Take only 500 years ago,—

what then was known of our present puny knowledge of the mystic sciences?

Unless the relationship between elements and forces is the basis of future scientific studies, science will, as it has done before, fall back and decline, become so filled with myths and erroneous theories as to become the greatest farce and absurdity. Science stands today at the forked road. If the right one is taken, science will advance; if the wrong one, then science will decline.

THE COLD-MAGNETIC DIVISION, EARTH'S PRIMARY FORCE. I have given this the name of The Cold Magnetic Division because the heat force is in no way associated with it.

The cold magnetic division is one of the divisions of the great central dual magnet. An explanation of it discloses and explains what the well-known phenomenon called gravity is. It shows the origin of gravity, also the point of its origin. All elementary matter at every opportunity gravitates towards the central magnet. Therefore the origin of gravity is one of the magnetic forces emanating from the great central magnet, and its point of origin is the frictional line between the earth's solid crust and the central molten matter, and not the earth's actual center as stated in our present-day scientific teachings. The actual center of the earth is a vacuum. How large, I cannot say.

It is the power of the attraction of the central magnet which causes matter at every opportunity to take steps in an endeavor to get nearer to the magnet. Thus matter gravitates towards it, therefore: the cold division of the central dual magnet is The Force of Gravity.

The sun's forces are neutral and in no way affinitive to the cold magnetic division. Nor do the sun's forces in any way affect it or its workings. Earthly elements are not affected in any way by the sun's forces. They are under absolute control in their movement of the cold magnetic division. This force extends its influence to the last particle of atmosphere on the edge of space. The influences of the cold magnetic force is over elementary matter only. It is neutral to forces generally. I might say one exception only, and there it is antagonistic. The cold magnetic force is ever attracting and drawing elementary matter towards itself—the central magnet; only when density intervenes is its further progress stopped. When the progress of matter is stopped by density, the central magnet then anchors it to the spot where it stops. There it remains until another opportunity occurs for it to move again towards the magnet.

The central magnet, according to various calculations made by scientists, who have made a study of the probable thickness of the earth's crust, seems to be about 45 to 50 miles below the earth's surface. I have never personally made any calculations, depending on what I find written. Their figures seem to be correct from phenomena which I have studied for a distance of about 20 miles down. All movements of matter must therefore be towards this 45–50 mile line.

The downward movement of matter is assigned to the force of gravity, which is correct. I cannot find, however, that any of our scientists have attempted to explain what the force of gravity is that carries matter down, or either to show where and how it originates.

A force is that which moves matter (not that every movement of matter is the work of the force of gravity). The force of gravity is one of nature's tools to move elements in a definite direction, namely, towards the central magnet. Also to prevent the outer division of the earth's centrifugal force from carrying any elementary matter out into space.

Gravity is the working of the cold magnetic division of the central magnet. The central magnet has two antagonists: first, the outside division of the earth's centrifugal force; and second, density. Density is not active but only resistive, yet gravity is responsible for the earth's density from the Archaean rocks to her surface. Even the atmosphere is affected by the cold magnetic force; as this is apparent in itself, it needs no explanation.

I shall now give a few illustrations of the working of the cold magnetic force showing the force of gravity, taking first Newton's theory as to why an apple falls to the ground.

I have selected this phenomenon for two reasons: First, because it is an example where the workings of the forces are distinctly those of the cold magnetic division only; second, because it is such a popular theme.

Why does an apple fall from the tree? Many moons ago that great scientist Sir Isaac Newton answered this question by saying that, "It was the attraction of the big body over the small one."

In some cases Sir Isaac would be partially true, but not with the apple. The falling of the apple is entirely due to the influence of the central magnet. The earth's elementary body has nothing to do with it. The earthly elements could not pull the apple down. It requires a force. Elements are not forces, but they are permeated with forces.

While the apple is still unripe, it clings to the tree. The running sap gives it an adhesive power, which is one of nature's provisions for bringing fruit to maturity. When the sap ceases to flow into the apple, a line at the end of the stem of the apple dries out and severs the connection. Then the adhesive power is gone. Then the cold magnet force calls upon the apple to make a start for the central magnet. The power of the magnet severs whatever is left of the dried-out fibers and pulls the apple from the tree to the ground. This may be considered by some as not being conclusive, in that it was not the elementary body of the earth that pulled the apple down. To make it conclusive and beyond controversy, I shall give an illustration of an apple tree on the side of a hill with the apples falling.

When the apples A.A. are pulled down by the central magnet, they strike the ground at B.B. From there they roll down the slope to C.C., where density intervenes and stops their further progress towards the central magnet.

The apple and all other matter will keep rolling towards the central magnet until stopped by density.

If, as Newton claimed, it was the attraction of the large body over the small body that pulled the apple down, then, when the apples touched the ground at B.B., they should have remained there, as they were in contact with the big body, but they do not. They go rolling down the hill until they are stopped by density at C.C., thus clearly showing that it was not the big elementary body that caused the apples to fall, but the force that made them roll from B.B. to C.C., which was the magnetic power of the central magnet.

Next I shall take up the subject of the attraction of a big body over a small one, and, as an example, will take a particle of dust clinging to a wall. All matter carries and is permeated with magnetic force. All forces, at all times, endeavor to join and aggregate. The wall has a larger volume of the force than the particle of dust. When the particle of dust touches the wall which has a greater volume of force, the forces are attached to each other and adhere, and as the particle of dust cannot surrender its force, it is compelled to remain in contact with the wall.

The power of the forces in elementary matter to attract and draw to each other depends on density and proportions. It is necessary that the small body holds only a given volume of the force, otherwise the central magnet will interfere and prevent the aggregation, as an example:

Take a grain of sand and place it against the wall alongside the particle of dust. The sand will immediately fall to the floor. The volume of the force in the sand is sufficient to enable the central magnet to pull it down against the lesser volume in the wall.

Why does water flow over the bed of a river and on to the ocean? The water is in constant touch with the earth, which is the large body. If the large body is the magnet, it should hold the water stationary and prevent its flow. It does not. The water flows on to the ocean, which is the nearest point it can get to the central magnet.

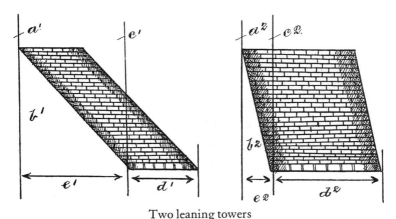

Two leaning towers

In these two towers, for the sake of illustration, densities are to be considered equal throughout all parts of both towers. Both towers are drawn out of perpendicular like the leaning tower of Pisa, Italy. The lines of centers of gravity C¹ and C² show the unequal divisions.

Fig. 1. This shows the greater part of the tower A^1 extending beyond its base line d^1—its overlap is shown by e^1. The pull of the central magnet being in proportion to each area shows that the magnetic pull is greater on e^1 than on d^1. The central magnet will pull this building down.

Fig. 2. This shows the area of E^2 to be less than d^2. This building will not fall because the magnet's pull on d^2 is greater than on E^2, the overlap. The line of center of gravity can be compared to the balance handle of a pair of scales. The side will dip and go down to the greatest weight, for weight is a measurement of the power of the cold magnetic force.

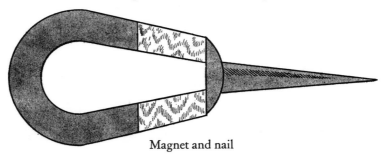

Magnet and nail

This is an exceedingly interesting example, as it shows the two divisions of the earth's primary force in antagonism against each other. Both are striving for the possession of the nail. The one endeavoring to aggregate and join two volumes of a magnetic force out of the electro-magnetic division, the other endeavoring to draw the elements composing the nail nearer to itself. Both the magnet and the nail have volumes of the same magnetic force in them, but the magnet being super-charged, has a great preponderance, as shown in the Fig. 1. The super-charged magnet has the nail in contact, as the nail is seen adhering to it. Although in contact, the force is not drawn out of the nail,—if it were, the nail would fall from the magnet. The magnet will hold the nail at any angle against the efforts of the cold magnetic force, provided the body of the nail does not have an area of surface and density where the cold magnetic force becomes stronger than the electro-magnetic force. The result depends entirely on the surface area and density of the nail.

If the nail is retained by the magnet, it shows that the electro-magnetic force overpowers the cold magnet. If, however, the nail falls as shown in the following cut, then clearly it is demonstrated that the cold magnetic force overpowers the electro-magnetic.

MAGNET AND NAIL
The electro-magnetic force surrendering the nail to the cold magnetic force

THE EARTH's CENTRIFUGAL FORCE. In addition to the earth's great primary force, she generates other forces which I have called secondary forces. Secondary because they originate from the primary force in combination with affinitive forces of the sun. The sun's forces are affinitive to certain forces in the electro-magnetic division of the earth's primary force.

The earth's centrifugal force is one of the two secondary forces about which there is much that can be said. This force is generated by the spin of the earth upon her axis. For convenience in explaining its workings, I shall make two divisions of it—the inside and the outside. The outside division works on the outside of the earth's crust, and the inside within the crust.

Were it not for the work of the outside division, the earth's cold magnetic force would hold everything down so tightly to the earth's surface that not a thing could move upon it, and the atmosphere would become so dense that nothing could breathe it. The outside division is therefore antagonistic to the influences of the central magnet. The central magnet endeavors to anchor all matter down to the earth's surface hard and fast, at the same time the centrifugal force is endeavoring to throw everything movable on the face of the earth out into space. The neutral zone of these two forces is the outside edge of the earth's atmosphere. The inside division works within the crust of the earth, and plays a very important part in the movements of the North Pole: and, it was an important factor in the shaping and development of the earth.

The earth's development has depended on the working out of the primary rock, the old Archaean gas chambers. Their elimination depended on the over-compression of gases in them, and, over-compression depended on the central centrifugal force driving the central gases out into the chambers through the various cracks and fissures which developed during the cooling and contraction of the primary rock. It has much to do with the movements of the north pole, as with the aid of the gyroscopical force, it accumulates and concentrates a super-volume of the magnetic forces in the polar regions, magnetic forces which have affinities in some of the sun's forces.

A centrifugal force is limited only in power by the size, density, and velocity of the revolving body generating it.

Velocity to a great extent is governed by the density of the revolving body, and the power which is revolving it.

As illustrations of the power of centrifugal forces constantly are seen instances where grindstones and metallic fly-wheels are burst asunder by their centrifugal forces and oftentimes with dire results. Yet, the volume of the forces which burst these wheels asunder are infinitesimal. The earth's centrifugal force, which is trying all the time to hurl us all out into space, is billions upon billions of times greater and more powerful than the puny forces emanating from grindstones and fly-wheels.

Although of such incalculable power, and although we are living in the midst of it, we cannot feel the earth's centrifugal force, because we are neutral to it, it is an extreme to the human body, and although of such incalculable power, it cannot hurl us off into space, because the magnetic force is more potent and holds us back.

All forces are silent in their movements. All sounds which we may hear through their workings or movements, such as thunder, are caused by the elements which they are affecting.

The question was recently put to me: Why does not the earth's great centrifugal force, the mere skin that forms her solid matter burst open this shell? A centrifugal force will burst a metal fly-wheel and grindstones, as we know from experience. That the earth's crust is but a very thin skin, when compared with her total diameter, all must admit. Comparatively speaking, not one thousandth part as thick as the shell on a fowl's egg. Yet the earth's crust does not bend or bulge out anywhere under the strain of her centrifugal force—why? This is a very easy question to answer, but, first I must say as I have previously stated, forces are so arranged that they are, in many cases, working against other forces and in all cases they form neutral zones, or one has the complete mastery over the other. Then the weaker one becomes non-effective—the earth's centrifugal force is non-effective against the tremendously greater power of the great central magnet. For while the centrifugal force in endeavoring to burst the crust of the earth and to throw everything on the face of the earth out into space, it cannot do this because of the stronger and more potent central magnet which overpowers the centrifugal force and draws all elementary matter towards itself at all opportunities. Density only stops matter rolling towards the magnet, and yet, the magnet is responsible for the density of the rocks above granite and the gneisses. To illustrate the excessive power of the magnet over the centrifugal force, throw a stone into the air. If the centrifugal force were stronger than the magnet, it would carry it off into space. But no, as soon as the magnet overcomes the temporary impetus given to the stone, it has full control over it, and quickly draws it to the surface of the earth, where it can go no further—density prevents it.

Now a question arises of what use is the earth's centrifugal force, for, nature has never been prodigal in her works. Therefore the centrifugal force was created for a purpose. What was that purpose? For one thing, it was to govern the density of the atmosphere, for, without the centrifugal force exerted to throw the atmosphere outwards, the central magnet would draw it all to the surface of the earth and there so compact it that nothing could breathe it, or nothing could live in it.

THE GYROSCOPICAL FORCE. The second secondary force is the earth's: gyroscopical force. This force is also generated by the spin of the earth on her axis.

The principal function of the gyroscopical force is to keep the earth in an upright position, and to prevent the sun from completely rolling her around from north to south. The sun's affinitive magnetic forces are, at all times, endeavoring to draw the earth's north pole in a direct line with herself. The earth's gyroscopical force is always working against it, trying to keep the north pole in its true or mean position. The gyroscopical force is therefore antagonistic to the sun's magnetic affinitive forces. As before stated, the electro-magnetic division of the central magnet is also antagonistic; without these antagonisms the earth's poles could not oscillate, neither could the earth revolve on her axis, phenomena which will hereafter be explained under the headlines: "The Earth's Spin" and "The Earth's Pendulum."

Chapter III. The Atmosphere

Wᴎɪʟᴇ it is not generally appreciated to be so, the fact remains that our atmosphere is very highly specialized. It is only during recent years, since the advent of radio, that the essence in which the popular atmosphere floats has been recognized as playing a most important part in the earth's welfare; and, further, it is not yet appreciated that the essence in which the atmosphere floats is an essence totally different to that which fills space. The essence in which the atmospheric particles float is under direct control of the central magnet, while that which fills space is in no way affected by the central magnet, as the magnet has no power over it whatever.

Although our scientists have never appreciated the foregoing facts, they were perfectly well known and understood by the scientists of the earth's first great civilization more than 50,000 years ago. They laid great stress upon it in their writings.

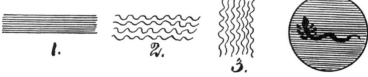

Naacal vignettes in the sacred writings of Mu

Our scientists assume that that which fills space, and that in which our popular atmosphere floats, is one and the same thing. It is not, as shown in the sacred inspired writings of the Motherland.

The ancients called that in which our atmosphere floats "the essence" and that which fills space they called "the water." In the ancient writings it is repeatedly pointed out that the light force is carried in the essence, and not in the particles of our popular atmosphere.

In the ancient writings the symbol for that which fills space was a series of fine horizontal lines, Fig. 1, which they wrote "water." The earthly water symbol was a serpent in motion, like the swells of an ocean, generally written as a series of wavy horizontal lines, Fig. 2. Why in ancient writings of 3000 or 4000 years ago call Fig. 1 "water"?

I think the symbol answers the question. The translators of the sacred writings could find no name corresponding with the original, to give to the plain horizontal lines, but the horizontal wavy lines were well known to them, so they differentiated between the two by calling one the "water" and the other "the waters." I have never found a word giving the name used by the ancients, only the symbol; but, their writings distinctly tell us that it is that which fills space. Not once but dozens of times.

In many of the vignettes of the sacred inspired writings is unquestionably shown what the fine straight horizonal lines symbolize. As an instance, when the Creator is spoken of as having existed in space, a vignette accompanying the writing shows the seven-headed serpent moving along through fine horizontal straight lines within a circle. Fig. 4.

LIGHTNING. Lightning is the result of an accumulation and a concentration of a volume of the electro-magnetic division of the earth's primary force at some point or area in the atmosphere,—a volume over and above what the atmosphere can hold and carry in suspension. This accumulation is passing on its way to some other area in the atmosphere, or is returning to earth—nature's storehouse for it.

[63]

Lightning is a compound force, including most if not all of the forces composing the electro-magnetic division of the earth's primary force.

The presence of lightning is revealed to us by a vivid incandescence in the atmosphere in the form of streaks popularly called "flashes of lightning."

This incandescence is not the force itself, but the superheated atmosphere along the line of its course. The accumulation may be of spherical form, or the form of a stream. Which it is, I have been unable to determine.

I have tried to measure the temperature of lightning, but have gained no satisfactory results.

An interesting point about lightning is that the flashes appear to be subject to variation in temperature dependent on in what direction the force runs. The flashes which run parallel to the surface of the earth or with an upward tendency appear to have the lowest temperatures. Those taking a downward course, making directly for the earth, have the highest temperature. This may possibly be due to the comparative density of the atmosphere.

I am giving two pictures of lightning flashes. One where the force is returning directly to the earth, A, and the other where the force is equalizing in the atmosphere and does not return to earth, B.

Picture A represents what is popularly called "fork lightning." The force is returning to earth from the point of concentration. During its passage through the lower areas of the atmosphere, portions of the bolt detached themselves. These portions show themselves in the photograph as rootlets running from the descending bolt. These parts are leaving the parent bolt to equalize in the atmosphere. The bolt is passing through an area which is slightly below in its holding capac-

Lightning. The earth's primary force being drawn back to the earth,
a volume over and what the atmosphere can hold in suspension

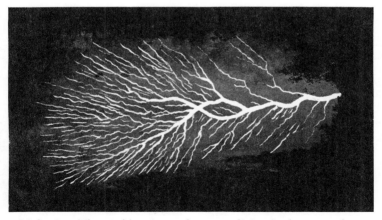

Lightning. The earth's primary force equalizing in the atmosphere

ity: these additions will bring this area of atmosphere up to its full holding capacity and equal with the surrounding areas.

The fact that these little streams of the force are leaving the mother bolt, shows in itself that the atmosphere in this area was below normal. After the atmosphere along the course of the bolt has been fully charged, the balance enters its storehouse—the earth, and there becomes dispersed.

In some areas, as will be seen in the picture, some large branches leave the mother bolt, indicating that where these branches shoot out, the atmosphere is exceedingly low in force. If a human being were placed in one of these denuded areas, virtual pockets, he would experience great difficulty in breathing and in his heart action, followed by numbness, and if the pocket were a large one he might even become unconscious of his surroundings. The cause would be the absence of the life force, the power that works his material machinery. There is a close relationship between lightning and the life force, because the life force is one of the compounds that enter into the makeup of lightning.

Picture B. This is an illustration of a flash of lightning running horizontally across the heavens.

This picture is copied from a photograph of an actual flash of lightning. The bolt started in the north and coursed along in a southerly direction. It was the most beautiful and awe-inspiring sight I have ever looked upon. The photo does not show its full length and fails utterly in disclosing its magnificence.

As the bolt passes on, innumerable branches and rootlets leave the mother bolt. These continue to leave the bolt until the bolt is entirely dissipated.

Here the forces are shown passing from a super-charged area to a practically denuded one. By drawing the surplus

[67]

forces from an overcharged area into the undercharged one, the forces become equalized in both areas.

Except in violent storms, when the forces equalize in the atmosphere it takes the form of what is popularly called "summer lightning" and sometimes "sheet lightning." These apparent sheets are made up of infinitesimally small bolts or streams, each one independent of each other. In this sheet form only exceedingly small vacuums are formed, so small that to the ear no sounds of thunder accompany it.

For many years I have known that equalizing of the earth's primary force went on in the atmosphere, and that its final working was in the form of minute flashings from one atmospheric particle to another, and from one minute area to another.

The major form of equalization, lightning, could be seen by its effect on the atmosphere. When, however, it came to the final interchanging, the flashings are so minute they cannot be detected either by the eye or photography. These flashings and equalization have been proven by the radio.

At times, harsh, crazy, squeaky sounds break in upon an opera star, or some very interesting lecturer. These sounds are of various degrees in intensity, sometimes drowning everything else. Radio fans now say "the static is interfering." As a matter of fact, they mean to express the exact opposite,—they mean "the static is being interfered with." Static means at rest. The crazy sounds are the result of unrest, therefore kinetic.

These sounds from the radio, whether they are mere scratchings or of ear-splitting intensity, are caused by movements of the earth's primary force in the atmosphere. Radio waves from the microphone to the receiver are formed in the essence, not in the popular atmosphere. The form of equalization of the force is by small streams or bolts. One particle of atmosphere holds much more force than the next one; the force in the overcharged one divides itself and a part leaves and jumps into the undercharged particle, thus equalizing the two.

But this little bolt has to cross a channel of essence in jumping from one atmospheric particle to another. Through this essence channel a radio wave is running; the bolt cuts through it and for a period of time less than a second breaks the wave. It is the breaking of the radio wave and the passage of the little bolt through the essence that produces the crazy sounds emitted by the radio.

The intensity of the crazy sounds is governed by the size of the bolt, the minimum being two particles of the atmosphere equalizing, and the maximum being an area. The intensity of the crash is governed by the size of the area, the greater the area involved the more intense will be the disturbance.

It is a well-known phenomenon among radio fans that greater distinctness and clearness of sound, with less atmospheric disturbance, is experienced at night and during winter months than during the hours of sunlight and summer months. This is a natural phenomenon. At night the sun's forces are not drawing the earth's forces from her body out into the atmosphere, there to be equalized. The only equalization going on at night is what has been incompleted during the day. There is no fresh supply drawn out during the night.

The same rule applies to summer and winter.

LIGHT. Before commencing to discuss the subject of light, let us first see what our prehistoric forefathers wrote about it.

The Sacred, Inspired Writings of Mu.

Section. The Creation.

Sub-section. The Third Command.

"Let the outside gases be separated and let them form the

[69]

atmosphere and the waters. And the gases were separated: one part went to form the waters, and the waters settled upon the face of the earth, and covered it, so that no land appeared anywhere. The gases that did not form the waters formed the atmosphere, and:

"The Light was contained in the atmosphere,

"And the shafts of the sun met the shafts of the earth in the atmosphere and gave it life. Then there was light upon the face of the earth."

Aitareya A'ram'ya. An ancient Hindu book. Slokas 4–8. "The atmosphere that contains the light."

Rig Veda. An ancient Hindu book. Pages 3–4. "He who measures out the light in the air."

The Nahuatl. From a Yucatan manuscript. "When One-yocax, the Creator who dwells in Himself, thought the time had come when all things should be created, He arose, and from His hands resplendent with light, He darted four arrows (the four great primary forces) which struck and put into motion the four elements that float in the atmosphere. The particles on being hit by the divine arrows became animated. . . . Then appeared the first rays of the rising sun, which brought life and joy throughout nature.

*   *   *   *   *   *

Light, heat and rays are so closely allied and intermingled that it becomes a difficult matter to speak of one without including the others. Light is a force. Heat is a force. But rays are not forces. They are the carriers of forces.

*   *   *   *   *   *

Light is an earthly force, a sub-division of the electro-magnetic division of the earth's primary force. The light force forms its waves in the essence in which the popular atmosphere floats.

When certain of the sun's affinitive forces which are carried in the light rays strike the earth's light force, which is held in suspension in the earth's atmospheric essence, it sets the earth's light force into movement, giving it life, as stated by the ancients. The movement of the force takes the form of waves. Each wave is made up of innumerable infinitesimally small sparks or flashes of the force.

Light travels through our atmosphere at the rate of 186,000 miles per second. Waves formed in the popular or analyzable part of our atmosphere are far too heavy and ponderous to travel at the rate of light, but the essence is so thin that this velocity is obtainable in it by the light force. At what rate the forces from the sun and other distant bodies pass through space, filled with an essence much thinner than that in which our atmosphere floats, I cannot say. Our distant stars are measured by light time calculated at 186,000 miles per second. How fast do the light forces travel through thin space? Much faster than here on earth without question. Therefore, it seems to me, the accepted distances of our distant suns are open for revision.

Between the sun's atmosphere and the earth's atmosphere the sun's rays are not seen. The space is a total darkness because there is no elementary matter in space to hold a light force in suspension. So the case stands: the male travels, the female waits. When they meet light results. One without the other is incapable of producing light.

That rays are not lost in space, although they pass through darkness and are not seen, is shown by the sun's rays coming into evidence again when they reach our atmosphere. This fact in turn is another proof that light is an earthly force:

because, if it came from the sun, it would be seen all through space from the sun to the earth. It also proves that the essence of our atmosphere is elementary, although we cannot analyze it.

It also proves that that which fills space is not elementary, or if it is, the earth's light force cannot be carried by it, neither our sun's or any other great sun's.

The eye can be excited in various ways so as to produce sight. It may be excited by the rude mechanical action of a blow. To produce vision, however, the eye must receive something coming from without. What is this something? In some way luminous bodies have the power of producing light. I have used the term "luminous bodies" because I think it will be better understood by the layman who has not studied this particular branch of science. As a matter of fact, however, no body is luminous. The body emits a parent ray which is dark and invisible, and leaves the body unseen. This ray is a compound ray of many colors. At a certain distance from the body, this dark invisible ray filters out the light rays which are apparent to vision. Thus between the light visible incandescent rays and the body emitting the rays, there is a dark space, which veils the body from sight, so that the body, not being seen, shows that it is not incandescent. In addition to the light rays, which become visible after they are filtered out from the parent ray, there remain ten times as many rays, which are not visible because they are ultra and intense "extremes."

Some time ago I came across a writing by a scientist stating that the flame of an electric light is composed of oxygen and hydrogen. This is not so. An electric light has no flame. That which appears to this scientist to be flames are rays only, about one-tenth of which sets the light force in the essence in motion, forming waves and producing the phenomenon of light.

Oxygen increases combustion. Combustion is flame when not smothered. If an electric bulb is broken at the time it is giving light, if it was emitting flames coming in contact with the atmosphere containing oxygen, the flames should materially increase. But do they? No! Directly the glass is broken the rays and so-called flames disappear, thus clearly proving that the electric light has no flame but rays only.

I will give two illustrations of parent rays being filtered in connection with combustion.

Fig 1.   *Fig 2*

A gas flame and candle flame

In both of these cases the parent ray assumes the form of an arc, around the point of the gas jet, and around the wick of the candle. Beyond the dark ray are the visible rays, flame. The distance from the body where the parent ray commences to the point where it filters out the light rays, is subject to great variation in different bodies. In some cases it is almost infinitesimal; in others, such as the illustrations shown, they are even measureable with the naked eye.

[73]

The parent ray commences to divide directly it comes into contact with the atmosphere, preparatory to the actual filtering out. It is very generally believed that light depends on heat, and that, in some manner, light and heat are one and the same thing. I shall hereafter conclusively show by experiments that: The light force does not contain one particle of heat, and that the heat force does not contain one particle of light.

I shall now take the human eye to show what vision is and how it is accomplished. I shall not attempt to give any details about the eye beyond what is necessary to show the parts of its machinery, so that the machine can be operated by the light force.

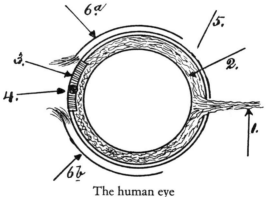

The human eye

The optician informs us that there is a nerve in the eye especially devoted to the purposes of vision called the optic nerve. This nerve emanates from the brain and passes from the brain to the back of the eye. There it divides into fine filaments, which are woven together into a kind of screen called the retina. The retina in front is covered by a movable shade which is called the iris. The iris is the colored part of the eye, such as blue, brown, and grey. In the center of this colored movable shade there is a small black spot, which is called the pupil.

The size of the pupil is the exposed area of the retina. The movements of the colored shade or iris are involuntary, over which no being has any control. It expands and contracts with the intensity of light. With the aid of the accompanying cut, I will turn the eye into a machine for the sake of easy explanation of its working, and show how the light force is the agent. We shall call the optic nerve the conduit, as it carries the force from the eye to the brain. The retina we shall call the receiver, because it is the retina that receives the force from without and carries it to the conduit. The colored iris we shall call the governor, because it controls the volume of the force taken in by the receiver, and the pupil we shall call the port, as all of the force has to pass into it.

The foregoing shows fairly well the machine which we shall now start working.

Light and vision result from a current of the light force, which takes the form of waves, each wave being made up of innumerable infinitesimally small sparks, flashes, or streams.

Each spark or flash in the wave strikes on the receiver, and by it the force is carried back to the conduit. Then the conduit conveys it to the brain, to certian lobes. Then vision is the result. Each tiny spark or flash in the wave, strikes a blow on delivery with the force contained in it, so that, with the continuous multiplicity of blows, and with their delivery of force, the current is never broken. This current of force continues as long as the ray exists, and as long as the current of force exists, vision remains. When the ray ceases, the current of force is broken. Then darkness prevails. It may be well to point out that when the ray gets shut off, there is a momentum in the force still left, which continues the wave and current for a time. Our twilight is the result of this momentum. In the case of artificial lights, such as fires, lamps, and candles, the momentum is so weak and short that it is not noticeable.

Light rays, those which are affinitive to and excite the light force, are all distinguishable to the eye, regardless of their color, and all rays regardless of the color that are palpable to vision, have the faculty of exciting the light force and causing light. The length of the spark in the light wave, the volume of the wave and its length, and the rapidity of its movements, are subject to variation, which variation governs the character of vision. And these variations are governed by the color of the ray which is carrying the force.

The wave formed from a white or an ultra intense red ray gives the most perfect vision, because the sparks in this wave are greater in volume and length and have a greater rapidity in movement than waves formed by any other colored ray. The length of a light wave formed by a white ray measures from about $1/50,000$th to $1/60,000$th part of an inch. The number of sparks in a wave cannot be realized. It is, however, clearly seen that the number of waves, with the innumerable sparks in each wave, each spark delivering its quota of force to the receiver with a blow, form a continuous, unbroken current of force, therefore producing a continuous, unbroken, unwavering light. A violet ray produces the weakest of all lights. Professor Proctor, writing on this subject, says: "The effect which we call color is due to the length of the light wave."

I disagree entirely with Proctor where he says: "Color is an effect." Proctor, like many other scientists, has made the mistake of placing the cart before the horse. Proctor makes the length of the wave responsible for the color, whereas the fact is the color is responsible for the length of the wave. Proctor apparently did not know that light is a force; consequently did not know whence light originates, or how it is generated. Light rays correspond with the colors shown in the spectrum: The spectrum does not record or disclose any of the dark rays. This I demonstrated and proved in a court of law in Europe, when as an expert witness I proved that temperatures cannot be measured by the spectrum. At the same time I demonstrated and proved that heat is carried in the dark invisible rays alone. Each colored ray or group of rays, both light and dark, whether they come from the sun or mechanical incandescence, affects the forces coming out of the electro-magnetic division of the earth's primary force. We are discussing the subject of light, so we shall see by a very simple experiment how the various colored rays affect the light force.

Take a series of glasses corresponding with the colors of the spectroscope, and, in addition, one that is pure white, and another very lightly tinted with red to represent intensity. Place each glass successively between a powerful incandescent lamp and some very fine printed matter. The distinctness of the print will depend on the volume and strength of the light force, falling on the print. Each glass will be an affinitive of its own colored ray, and will repel all other light rays. Each colored ray coming through the glass will carry a volume of the light force according to its capacity. On striking the print, the ray is deflected to the eye. Thus the clearness of vision is governed by the volume and rapidity of movement of the force carried in the ray. The white clear glass will give one extreme, and the mauve glass the opposite extreme. It is noticeable that waves of light formed by the primary colors are stronger than those formed of secondary colors.

If, as Proctor says, "Color is an effect," then all inanimate matter such as rocks, wood, foliage, and points must all be extremely radioactive, and especially so when we take into consideration that light rays only form about one-tenth of the whole. It is true that all matter is permeated with the electro-magnetic division of the primary force. Not all varieties of matter, however, are incapable of holding a sufficient volume of the force to become radio-active, only a very few. If all matter produced Proctor's "effect," then all matter would be so radio-active that the burning effects of radium would not be worth talking about. In fact we should not be able to talk, for we should all be shrivelled up. By increasing or intensifying a light ray, the volume, the rapidity of movement, and the size of the spark are increased.

A much larger area of the receiver is required to produce perfect vision when the current is weak than when the current is strong. For perfect vision, the receiver must deliver to the conduit its full carrying capacity, no more or no less. When too much current is delivered to the conduit, that is, more than it can convey, the movable shade or the governor involuntarily closes in and reduces the area of reception to balance the capacity of the conduit. As examples:

If we pass from a dimly lighted room having only an 8-candle power lamp into a brightly lighted room having a 100-candle power lamp, we find on entering the room that we are compelled for a short time partially to close our eyes to avoid what is popularly termed "glare." By thus partially closing the eye, the lids are partially drawn over the receiver, thus reducing its area of reception. The eyelids remain thus partially closed until the governor has acted by closing in over the area of reception itself. When the governor has adjusted the area of reception to the capacity of the conduit, the eyelids automatically open again to their normal extent.

On entering the brightly lighted room, we were compelled

to close our eyes partially, because we came from a low current of force into an intensified one. It was a greater volume of force than could be conveyed by the conduit. When we left the dimly lighted room, the receiver was calibrated for the current emanating from an 8-candle power lamp. When we entered the brightly lighted room, the receiver had to be re-calibrated to suit the force emanating from a 100-candle power lamp. On entering the brightly lighted room, a current of force struck the receiver, which was many times more than what the conduit could convey in its condition then. As soon as this condition was encountered, the receiver automatically commenced to re-calibrate itself, so that only as much force should be taken in as could be conveyed by the conduit without overflowing over the eye-ball. By reducing the receiving area of the receiver, the volume of force passing to the conduit is reduced; its character, however, is not changed.

An overflow of the conduit is demonstrated by the eye smarting and watering, causing what may be termed semi-blindness, or, an incapacity to see distinctly.

An overflow of the force is caused by the receiver taking in a greater volume of force than can be carried by the conduit to the brain, so that what is not taken by the conduit is spilled over the eyeball. I shall take a water pipe as an example: When the pipe is carrying its capacity and more is added, the addition spills over. Tears or watering of the eye is nature's remedy; the elementary parts of water are very affinitive to the force. The water collects the spilled force and carries it away from the eye in the form of tears.

When going from a brightly lighted room into a dimly lighted one, vision again becomes indistinct. The cause is the reverse to my first example, and all actions of the eye are reversed.

[79]

An examination of the eye discloses the fact that in a dimly lighted room the area of the receiver is large, and in a brightly lighted room small.

When the light is extremely bright, as is the case with furnace fires, colored glasses are used to protect the eyes. These glasses repel all light rays that do not partake of their own colors, thus reducing the current of force which strikes the eye.

I shall now examine the eyes of some night-seeing animals like the owl and the cat.

The eyes of an owl

THE OWL. The owl is one of the birds which can see perfectly and distinctly during the dark hours of the night only. From the foregoing cut of the owl's eyes, it will be seen that the eye has an enormous receiving area. The eye shows an extremely narrow iris or governor. In the owl the governor is not under control, nor does it work automatically like many other night-seeing animals. Therefore it cannot calibrate its receiver so as to see distinctly during the day or sunlight. Being unable to control the governor, a greater volume of the light force is taken in by the receiver during the day than can be carried by the conduit. An overflow of the force and semi-blindness is the result, so the owl sleeps during the day and works during the night. At night the enormously large receiver is capable of collecting a sufficient volume of the light force from the weak and ever-weakening current to fill out the capacity of the conduit. And, as the conduit is conveying its full capacity, the owl can see objects as clearly during the dark hours of the night as we can see them during the bright hours of the day.

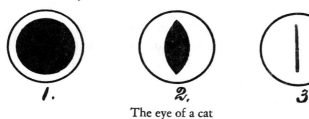

1.   *2.*   *3.*

The eye of a cat

THE CAT. The cat is a domesticated animal that can see as well during the dark hours of the night as during the bright hours of daylight. There is a difference between the eyes of the owl and those of a cat, which is: The owl has no control over the governor of the eye, whereas the cat has perfect control. In the cat's eye, the governor is capable of both great expansion and an equally great contraction.

Fig. 1. "During night light." This figure shows the condition of the cat's eye during the dark hours of the night, the governor is drawn back to its limit, exposing an enormous area of reception, corresponding with the receiver of the owl which only sees at night.

Fig. 2. "Subdued light." This figure shows the condition of the cat's eye during the hours of late twilight and early dawn. The iris, the movable shade or governor, is here shown drawn in over about one-half of the total area of the receiver, thus reducing the area of reception to about one-half, to take in only as much force as can be conveyed by the conduit.

Fig. 3. "Bright light." This figure shows the condition of the eye during the bright hours of day. The governor is here shown so drawn in that only a fine hair-like line of the receiver is left exposed, thus reducing the current of force received to the minimum.

Night-seeing birds and night-seeing animals thus demonstrate that vision, the power to distinguish objects, may continue after the body which has been emitting the light ray has disappeared and proving beyond all question that the light waves continue also, which in turn proves that there is a momentum left in the force which continues for a time. It is also shown that the momentum resulting from the forces of the sun continues throughout the night, but with ever-decreasing velocity and power. After the rays of the sun have left the atmosphere, the current of the earth's light force continues to move like a fly-wheel after the power driving it is shut off. The mechanical fly-wheel continues to revolve, but with ever-decreasing speed. Each turn or revolution becomes slower and slower until finally it stops, indicating that the earth's cold magnetic force has overcome the force of momentum and anchored the wheel. The cold magnetic force was enabled to accomplish this because momentum is only a weak temporary force. The lines of momentum are centrifugal in a wheel. The mechanical fly-wheel will not start revolving again until power is applied. So it is with the light force in the atmosphere. After the sun's ray with its affinitive forces has been shut off, which is the power, the energy of the light force in the atmosphere becomes weaker, hour after hour, until the hour just before the dawn when it is at its weakest ebb.

[82]

Man cannot see distinctly at night like the cat and the owl because the governor of man's eye is incapable of sufficient expansion to expose a sufficient area of the receiver to take in a volume of the weakened force sufficient to fill out the capacity of the conduit. Could the governor of man's eye be made to expand to an equal extent with those of the owl and the cat, then man like these animals would also see as distinctly at night as he does by day.

The foregoing opens up a very pretty and interesting moral lesson for us all.

HEAT. Our heat is an earthly force and does not come directly from the sun. I shall define what heat is:

Heat is a phenomenon which is a collection and a concentration of a sub-division of the electro-magnetic division of the earth's primary force at a given point or area, which the surrounding substances are incapable of carrying away by interchange and equalization at a sufficient rapidity to prevent a rise in the temperature at the given point or area.

What is temperature?

Temperature is the indication and measurement of a collection of the earth's heat force at a given point or area. The degree of temperature is the measurement of the volume of the force at the point or area.

The heat force—normally—is a cold force. It is in a cold condition during the time it is being held in reserve in the earth's storehouse for her forces, also in reserve in the atmosphere.

In any room of a building there is sufficient heat force held in reserve to melt the building, if the heat force in the room were brought up to its maximum degree of activity.

The action of the heat force is plainly told in the old Naacal tablets, "and the shafts of the sun met the shafts of the earth's

[83]

heat in the atmosphere, and gave it life, and the face of the earth was warmed by the heat," and again in the Nahuatl, "The particles being hit by the divine arrows became animated, and heat was developed." Affinitive forces of the sun are carried in his rays. The forces affinitive to the earth's heat force first draws it from the surface of the earth out into the atmosphere as shown in illustration on page 41. When in the atmosphere, the two forces, the earth's and the sun's, commingle and then the heat force becomes alive and takes the form of waves. As a matter of fact there are two of the sun's magnetic affinitive forces connected with the workings of the heat force. The first sun's force draws the cold heat force from the earth's skin out into the atmosphere. This sun's force does not animate the heat force and give it life. The heat force comes in contact with the animating force in the atmosphere only.

The sun's magnetic force, which draws the heat force from the earth's body is incapable of exciting it into activity to give it movement and life. This is apparent from the fact that the force leaves the earth's body in a cold state. If this particular magnetic force of the sun were capable of transforming the heat force into activity, it would do so before the force left the body of the earth, and as the earth's body is permeated with the heat force, it would bring about a condition: the condition would be, a red-hot surface to the earth upon which no life could exist. As the earth's surface is not red-hot, and as it is permeated with the heat force, which is being constantly drawn out by an affinitive force of the sun, it is clearly demonstrated that this drawing affinitive force is a different one to that which brings the force into life in the atmosphere.

I have previously stated that the atmosphere has a governed holding capacity of forces, that each atmospheric particle of the atmosphere whether it be the essence or the analyzable parts, can hold and carry in suspension just so much and no more. I shall now go further and say that this regulation applies to individual forces as well as the whole. Therefore it is thus shown that the sun's magnetic force, which draws the heat force from the earth's body, can draw just so much and no more. When the holding capacity for the heat force is filled, the magnetic force can draw out no more because there is nowhere to put it.

Fossils of vegetation have been found in the cold arctic regions of growths only found in tropical and super-tropical climates, showing that at the time when these plants were growing, our now frigid arctic regions were then hot or super-tropical. A very interesting question thus arises. What has become of the heat that in ancient times made our polar regions super-tropical?

Heat is a force that requires room-space in elements, and, as there are no elements in space beyond our atmosphere, it is self-evident that it did not wander out into space and there get lost.

At the time when the waters first settled upon the thin crust of the earth, there was insufficient storage for the forces in her body. Consequently a super-bulk was outside mixed in with the atmosphere. They were there awaiting storage accommodation. As the crust of the earth thickened, so the storage plant was increased, and, as this was increased, the over-charge in the atmosphere was gradually drawn in and stored. This resulted in the lowering of the heat force in the atmosphere, in ratio to the thickening and cooling of the earth's crust. At the beginning what is now our frigid regions were super-tropical, and as the crust of the earth thickened, so their temperatures went down until they became what they are now.

[85]

Space to all intents and purposes is a vacuum. The heat force can neither enter or pass through a vacuum. Space forms a complete barrier to the passage of the heat force in any direction. Space is nothingness, and the heat force cannot enter nothingness. Forces in a manner duplicate the workings of the elements, that is, they become tired out and exhausted after performing a service assigned to them by nature.

Elements when exhausted after performing some function assigned to them by nature, return to mother earth for regeneration and to be born over again. Leaves fall from the tree and bush, grasses mature and die down, thus they pass into nature's laboratory, where they decompose and return to the soil from whence they came, to be again, at some future date, taken up and formed into new vegetation. When forces become exhausted, they are drawn back by the great central magnet to the frictional line. There they are regenerated and passed out into the storehouse, the cold hard crust of the earth.

The exhausted heat force is thus regenerated and passed out into the storehouse. There it remains in a cold inanimate state until called upon by nature for some other work.

While the sun's forces are drawing volumes of the heat force from the earth's body in a regenerated condition, the earth's great central magnet is drawing back for regeneration an equal volume of tired out, exhausted force, thus following out the great law governing motion and life by forming a circular or orbital movement. I have heretofore laid great stress on the fact that the earth's cold hard crust is the storehouse of her regenerated forces. Now I wish to emphasize the following facts:

As the earth's crust thickened, so the temperatures surrounding the earth dropped.

The drop was in ratio to the thickening of the earth's crust.

When the heat force becomes tired out and exhausted, the sun's forces have no more power over it.

A controlling magnetic force cannot be stored in a super-heated body. The body must be cold.

A force cannot be regenerated in a cold area.

Various phenomena show that the reserve forces stored in the earth's body far exceed the volume of forces held in suspension in the atmosphere. Through this surplus in the earth's body a neutral zone was struck. This neutral zone is now instrumental in preventing the earth from solidifying and cooling any deeper. From the time this neutral zone was established, the temperatures of the earth's atmosphere were finally settled.

Today there is as great a volume of the heat force carried in the atmosphere of the frigid zones as there is in that of the tropical belt.

As soon as the heat force arrives in the atmosphere from the body of the earth, under a natural law, it commences to equalize in the atmosphere by interchange, that is, each particle of atmosphere has an equal volume of the force. What we know as radiation is nothing more than the interchanging and equalizing of the heat force throughout the area, a room or the open. When the force becomes exhausted again, it is claimed by the central magnet.

When out in the atmosphere, the sun's forces hold the earthly forces in suspension, including the heat force, until the day has passed and the sun has sunk below the horizon. From this moment the sun's forces have no power over the forces in the atmosphere. Then the great central magnet commences its work. It draws back to the frictional line all exhausted forces, and apparently those also that are in a very weakened condition. Gradually the momentum slows down,

[87]

and as it slows down, the forces become less active. Thus the phenomenon of night being colder than the day is explained. Another phenomenon is the earth experiences various temperatures at different parts of her surface, hot, temperate, and frigid. This condition is brought about by:

First—The angle at which the sun's rays cut the earth's lines of forces.

Second—The length of time during each day of the year that the sun's rays cut these lines of forces.

From this it is seen that both time and angles are involved; a natural law, however, is followed: The more direct the angle at which the sun's forces strike the lines of forces of the earth, the greater is the power of the sun's forces. Consequently, at these angles we find the maximum heat: the tropics.

At the angles at which the sun's rays become obtuse so that the effect of the sun's forces are lessened, here we find a milder temperature: the temperate regions.

Where the sun's rays strike the face of the earth at the most obtuse angles, we find the maximum frigidity: the polar regions. The accompanying illustration is an explanation:

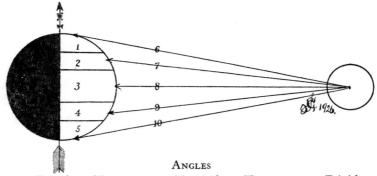

ANGLES

1—Frigid; 2—Temperate; 3—Tropical; 4—Temperate; 5—Frigid;
6—Most obtuse angles; 7—Obtuse angles; 8—Direct right angles;
9—Obtuse angles; 10—Most obtuse angles

[88]

I shall now give some well-known phenomena that will serve as proofs that the heat force requires room space in elements; without elements it could not exist.

If we raise the temperature, of say, a piece of iron, the iron will expand; the additional or rather added volume of force has made room for itself in the iron by expanding it. Then, if we withdraw the added heat by cooling the iron, the iron will shrink back into its original size. This is the common phenomenon known as expansion and contraction.

At night when the sun's rays are falling on the opposite side of the earth, we can again super-heat the iron and expand it. Do we get this heat from the sun, which is on the other side of the earth? Decidedly not. This heat is taken out of the atmosphere where it was lying dormant and cold, having been previously drawn from the earth's body, but not exhausted.

A common and a well-known phenomenon is that the nearer we get to the source of heat, the higher we find the temperature; as an example, there is a hot stove at the end of a long room. In the opposite end of the room we find the temperature many degrees lower than close around the stove. In the center of the room the temperature is about midway between the two ends of the room. Therefore if our heat comes from the sun, as our scientists tell us it does, the nearer we get to the sun, the warmer we should find it. Do we? Let us see.

We will go to the tropics for there we shall find the sun directly above our heads. We will start from the shores of the ocean—sea level. We register the temperature and find it to be 110° F. We take a balloon and rise 10,000 feet in a direct line to the sun; at this elevation we find the temperature has dropped down to freezing point, 32° F. We take another jump up to 40,000 feet above sea level, still heading direct for the sun. We are now several miles nearer to the sun than at sea level. We register the temperature again. It has dropped to 50° below zero. The cold is unbearable, yet scientists tell us that 40,000 feet above sea level we are that much nearer the source of heat.

To corroborate the results of our balloon ascent, let us do a little mountain climbing. We will make our start from a warm valley at the base of a high mountain. As we ascend this mountain, we find that it grows colder and colder. This clearly proves that the higher we ascend from sea level, so the temperature is proportionately lowered. And, as we leave the earth's surface, so we are leaving the source of the earth's heat.

Another well-known phenomenon is that as we ascend from sea level, so the atmosphere becomes proportionately less dense. It rarifies as we go up. This phenomenon is that there are fewer atmospheric particles to the cubic inch 10,000 feet up than there are at sea level. This diminution of atmospheric particles is not always in regular ratio as shown by G. L. Tanzer in "Cosmic Reciprocity."

Two facts now confront us:

The first is, as we ascend from sea level, the atmosphere becomes more rarified. That is, there are fewer atmospheric particles to the cubic inch floating in the essence. The second is, each atmospheric particle can hold a given quantity only of the heat force.

There is the reason why the temperature drops as we ascend from sea level. I will reduce it to a sum in arithmetic. At sea level there are 10,000 particles of atmosphere to the cubic inch registering a temperature of 110° F. At 10,000 feet altitude we find only 5000 (?) particles to the cubic inch. These can only hold half the volume of the force. Therefore the temperature should be one-half of what it is at sea level. We find this is so, for at the 10,000 foot elevation, the temperature has dropped to 55° F. The foregoing figures are only given as a basis on which to form an example. The actual figures may be found in most scientific works.

What further proof is required to show that the earth's heat does not come from the sun, but is one of her own forces?

I shall next take up an example of a totally different character, the workings of a thermo-electric pyrometer.

HEAT PHENOMENA. A sufficient volume of the heat force accumulated and concentrated at a given point is capable of producing thermo-chemical reactions—analyses.

A thermo-chemical analysis is the undoing of a previous thermo-chemical synthesis. A thermo-chemical synthesis, which we may be analyzing today, may have been formed tens of millions of years ago. There are various mechanical ways and means by which the heat force may be accumulated and concentrated, both mechanically and chemically. It is, however, easier to accumulate and concentrate many of the forces of the electro-magnetic division of the primary force than to isolate and concentrate the heat branch alone. This being the case, it is the general custom to accumulate an affinitive group of which heat forms one, or maybe the light force forms one also.

The dynamo, which is a piece of mechanical machinery, does not generate the electro-magnetic force. The dynamo only draws the force out of the surrounding atmosphere, where it is being held in suspension. The atmosphere surrounding the dynamo cannot be denuded of the forces; interchange and equalization prevents it. As the dynamo cuts the lines of the forces and diverts them into its own channels, surrounding forces follow in and keep the atmosphere fully charged with a constant current coming from the earth's body to replace all forces that become exhausted. The heat force has an affinity for all elements, some strong, others weak, and some almost, but not quite, negative. The greatest elementary affinity of the heat force is oxygen. Friction, which is neither an element or a force, but a phenomenon resulting from the workings of elements and forces, has the faculty of collecting and concentrating the heat force. Earthly surface frictions are minute duplications of the workings of the great central magnet. Sufficient friction will accumulate and concentrate such a volume of the heat force as to enable it to cause combustion and burn up solid bodies. Flames of fire are the result of a thermo-chemical analysis. A thermo-chemical analysis from the result of friction may cause a solid to be transformed and pass off into the atmosphere in the form of super-heated gases. The phenomenon is commonly called "flames of fire." After the analysis of a compound has been started by mechanical friction, the further friction which carries on the analysis owes its existence to chemical friction caused by the separating of the elements of the compound forming the solid. For all thermo-chemical separations are accompanied by chemical friction. This chemical friction continuously accumulates and concentrates further volumes of the heat force in the compound that carries on and continues the combustion.

A thermo-chemical analysis can be accelerated by the use of oxygen.

Friction in itself is incapable of starting or maintaining a flame of fire, for, like the dynamo, it is only the agent which collects and concentrates the force. The force, and the force only, is responsible for the flame. As soon as the fire starts, the volume of the force which started it passes on in the flame into the atmosphere and there proceeds to equalize. It is this particular form of equalizing that warms the atmosphere surrounding a fire. After the fire is exhausted, the equalizing of the force continues and extends until the atmosphere around where the fire stood becomes normal, for, under the great law of equalization, the interchanging must continue until the force becomes equally distributed throughout and around where the fire stood, just as the waters of an ocean after a storm level off, and the surface becomes equalized.

The foregoing explanation of heat accounts for another well-known phenomenon — that of smothering or putting out a fire by cutting off the atmospheric draughts from it, lowering the intensity of a fire by reducing the atmospheric draughts, or increasing the intensity of the fire by increasing the atmospheric draughts. It is not the atmosphere or any of the elements composing the atmosphere that is primarily responsible for the changes in the intensity of the fire; the changes are solely due to the volume of force. The force is primary, the elements composing the atmosphere are auxiliary, as one of the agents—oxygen—carries or brings the heat force in. As before stated, the atmosphere holds vast volumes of forces in suspension; every atom or particle of oxygen carries its quota of the heat force. Therefore, as the volume of the atmospheric draughts is reduced or increased, so in proportion is the volume of the force which is being supplied to the chemical friction either increased or reduced. By cutting off all atmospheric draughts, the supply of force to carry on the burning is cut off, and the fire can continue no longer.

I have made the statement that heat is an earthly force and followed this statement with various well-known phenomena showing how the force works. I shall now demonstrate and reasonably prove that heat is a force, also an earthly force. For this purpose I shall call to my assistance what is known as the thermo-electric pyrometer.

A thermo-electric pyrometer is designed for measuring

[93]

temperatures, especially high temperatures. From personal experience and tests which I have made, I can say that accurate measurements can be made with it up to about 2000° F. Beyond this point it does not record accurately on account of the critical point in the metal forming its fire end. An approximate reading can be made beyond 2000° F., but it can only be approximate.

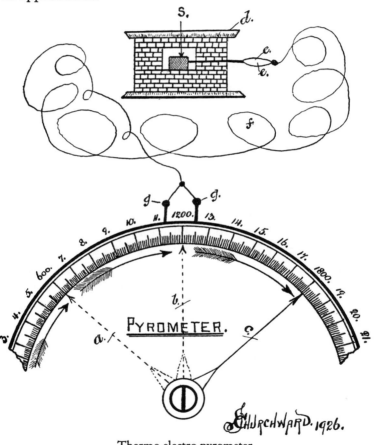

Thermo-electro pyrometer

As a matter of fact, the thermo-electric pyrometer does not record heat any more than does the prism. The pyrometer measures and records the volume of the magnetic current, not the heat current. The heat and magnetic forces which affect the pyrometer are branches of the electro-magnetic division of the primary force, and except when they are purposely isolated from one another, they are associated, but always in an exact proportion one to the other. This rule never varies. Thus if we fix the volume of the magnetic force as $x = 100°$ F. of heat, we also find that $2x = 200°$ F., and $3x = 300°$ F., and so on up to 2000° F.

My usual manner of calibrating my thermo-electric pyrometer was with hot water. Bring the water up to 100° F. as shown by an ordinary thermometer. Then immerse the fire end in the water and calibrate it to read 100° F. Then as a check-off run the water up to 200° F. as shown by the thermometer, and test the thermo-electric to see if it is reading accurately.

Very few laymen know the construction and workings of a thermo-electric pyrometer, so I have made a drawing of one in connection with a piece of hot steel in a furnace, and with this drawing I give an explanation, which I feel sure will be understood by everyone reading it. (See page 94.)

D, the furnace. S, the hot steel. F, a pair of ordinary insulated wires. E, a detachable joint called the fire end, made of some refractory metal such as platinum-platinum-rhodium or platinum-iridium. E.E, connection of fire end with lead wire outside of the furnace. G.G, connection of the other end of the lead wire with the pyrometer.

Thus it is seen that from the pyrometer P to the furnace D, containing the hot steel S, whose temperature is being measured, runs a pair of ordinary insulated wires F, the same kind of wires as are used for lighting purposes. These wires are connected outside the furnace at E.E with the fire end also composed of two wires but of refractory metal. The other end of the fire end rests against the hot steel S. At the other end of the lead wire which may be of any length from 100 feet to a mile, a connection is made with the pyrometer at G.G. In the instrument the current is transferred to a coil, then on to the needle or indicator, which it moves forward or backward as the current may vary. The needle point is on a dial divided into degrees. Thus the movement of the needle points to a degree in the current which in turn gives the degree of temperature or what the volume of the heat force is which is lodged in the body of the steel in the furnace. This outline shows all positions and conditions. It will be seen that any electric current that may move the needle or indicator, in either direction, forwards or backwards, must come from the steel in the furnace as the pyrometer is in connection with nothing else.

Having given an outline of the instrument and the manner of its working, I shall now put it into operation.

The ingot is placed in the furnace at atmospheric temperature, say 70° F. The needle will be pointing to the 70-degree mark on the dial. The next step is what is technically termed "fire the furnace," i.e., turn on the heat. As the ingot begins to absorb the heat, it delivers the electric current to the fire ends; these through the lead wires deliver it to the pyrometer. The force then passes through the coils and advances the needle from 70° to 600°, marked A on the instrument, showing that now there is an accumulation of heat in the ingot which raises its temperature to 600° F.

Now open up more draughts and thus increase the intensity of the fire. The ingot absorbs more of the heat force and the needle proceeds to show the increase by moving from the 600° point to the 1200° point, marked B on the face of the instrument. Let another set of draughts be opened up equal to each of the first and second. The needle advances until it arrives at the 1800° mark and there stops at C on the face of the instrument. There are now 1800 units of the magnetic force in the ingot which tells us that there is also 1800° F. of the heat force.

By "drawing the fire," that is, cutting off all of the draughts, a reaction takes place, the needle is seen moving back, showing that the forces are leaving the ingot. The rate of the needle's progress is governed by the rapidity with which the forces leave the body of the ingot, and interchange with the surrounding atmosphere and substances. This form of interchange and equalization is commonly called cooling.

A pyrometer should always be placed at a spot where the temperature is normal, and as far away from the substance whose temperature is being measured as possible, so that no radiated heat coming from the furnace can affect it to cause a false registration of temperature of the substance being measured. It is also clearly demonstrated that it can only be a force coming from the ingot that affected the instrument, and that it was a magnetic force and not the heat force.

It has now been shown that as the temperature of the steel ingot was raised, it was accomplished by atmospheric draughts, which carried in volumes of the heat force accompanied by a magnetic force. The magnetic force was carried to the instrument and moved the needle, the movements of the needle all the time corresponding to the increased volume of forces being concentrated in the ingot.

It may, however, be argued, that the elements composing the atmospheric draughts were the responsible agents which raised the temperature of the ingot. To meet such an argument and to check the foregoing, I will make another test. This time in an electric furnace, where draughts are not used. An electric furnace is as near a vacuum as is possible to get. The agent for melting the steel will be what is known as an electric current, which contains the main branches of the electro-magnetic division of the primary force. In this case the heat force is accumulated and concentrated in the steel unaided by any atmospheric draughts. As the forces accumulate in the steel, the temperature continues rising until the metal breaks down and melts. A thermo-chemical analysis has commenced. Melting is the first step. This demonstrates that it was the heat force and the heat force alone that raised the temperature of the steel ingot to 1800° F. in the first experiment.

Before closing this section on heat, I shall add a few words more about friction.

Friction is not a force. Friction is nature's agent for the accumulation and concentration of forces. Example:

Take two pieces of wood and rub them violently one against the other. In a short time the wood will ignite and burst into flame. The fire does not emanate from the hand working the sticks, nor is the necessary volume of the force contained in the sticks, otherwise the sticks would ignite without rubbing.

Friction is the greatest affinitive of the heat force, so that wherever friction is produced, heat will be collected and concentrated. With the grinding of the sticks one against the other, the friction goes on until a sufficient volume of the heat force is collected at the point sufficient to start combustion. The hands and the pieces of wood are like the dynamo, only agents in collecting and concentrating the force.

Chapter IV. Rays

I HAVE already discussed rays to a great extent in the two preceding chapters. There are, however, many points connected with rays which have not yet been brought forward.

The universe is made up of elements and forces.

Most of the elements are apparent to vision.

None of the forces can be seen by the human eye.

Elements and forces are indispensable to each other. All movements of elements are made through the agency of forces.

If there were no elements, then only the supreme force could exist.

Without the forces the elements would be dead and immovable.

All earthly elements emit rays.

Forces do not emit rays.

Some elements emit visible rays at high temperatures only, while others emit them at low temperature. In some cases temperature is in no way responsible for the rays.

All forces emanating from the sun, and all forces coming out of the electro-magnetic division of the primary force, are carried and transported in rays. All rays are carriers of forces; the rays themselves are not forces but only the carriers of the forces. This is similar to a pitcher of water, the pitcher is not the water, only the carrier of it.

Super-heated bodies emit rays. A super-heated body is red, yet while the body remains red, it may appear to be white or straw in color, on account of its light rays which surround it. A colored visible ray may become so intensified as to become invisible.

The vari-colored rays, the light-visible rays, are not due to any change in the color of the body emitting them, because when they leave the body they are dark invisible parent rays. Their various colors are due to the dividing up and filtering out each separate ray from the parent ray by our specialized atmosphere. When any particular ray has been filtered out, it becomes the carrier of some particular force. Looking into a fiery furnace, we never see the actual body emitting the rays. We only see the halo formed by the light visible rays, after

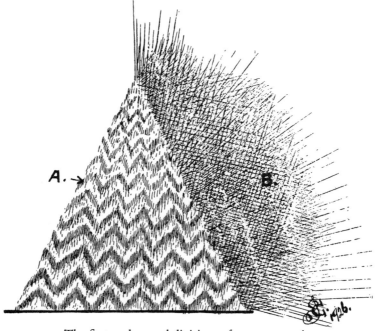

The first and second divisions of a parent ray in
which colors appear

they have been filtered out from the parent rays, and then only before they become dispersed in the atmosphere. To see the body itself, the light rays must be veiled and the halo eliminated.

Could the human eye distinguish the dark rays as it can the light rays, all breathing animals would appear as living within a halo.

The dark invisible parent ray first breaks into a pyramidal zig-zag form of wave (A, page 101). These zig-zags have the colors of the spectrum. This I believe to be a dividing out between the light and dark rays. From these zig-zags the final filtering takes place in the form of fine straight lines (B, page 101), of all colors, and as they shoot out, so the wave is reduced, until finally it disappears entirely; the colored rays

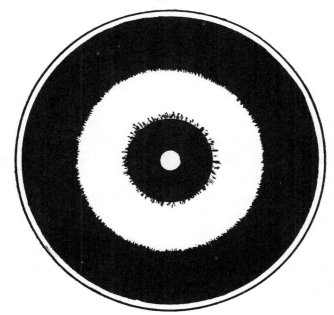

Cross section of an electric bulb

can only be traced for a short distance from the pyramid, then they get lost to the eye in the atmosphere.

Although I have stated that the parent ray assumes the form of a zig-zag pyramid, it is absolutely impossible to say whether this pyramidal form commences directly the parent ray leaves the body or whether it travels some distance before it commences to form, because no parent ray can be seen on leaving its source. Not until the light rays begin to be divided out from the dark ones, can any ray be seen. It is quite possible that the parent ray may assume some other form before showing the zig-zag pyramid.

To illustrate my previous statement "that we never see the actual body that is emitting the rays," I have selected an electric incandescent lamp for an example. The film which is emitting the light is only as thick as a fine hair. By carefully measuring the diameter of the halo of light rays around the film in a medium kilowat bulb, it is found to be fully ⅛ of an inch in diameter, several hundreds of times the diameter of the body emitting the rays. We see the rays, but we cannot see the actual film.

In the electric incandescent light there are no flames,—it is purely rays. Flames require to be fed with oxygen; the bulb is a vacuum with no oxygen, therefore the necessary adjunct to actual flames is not present.

There are many peculiar phenomena connected with rays; one is that different bodies emit the same colored rays at vastly different temperatures.

The burning end of a cigar emits a cherry-red ray at 600° F. Steel emits the same ray at 1200° F. An incandescent lamp with a carbon filament emits a straw-colored ray; remove this bulb and put one in its place with a tungsten filament, and a white ray is emitted.

The flame of a tallow candle emits a straw-colored ray. The flame of a refined wax candle a white ray.

Fire-flies and glow worms emit a white ray. The temperature of these insects is under 100° F. Yet to get the same colored ray from steel, a temperature of from 1800° F. to 2000° F. is required.

I can form a gas from certain elements that when lit burns with a pure white ray, yet the temperature of the flame is under 100° F. (atmospheric temperature). The flame will pass through the fingers and hands without any sensation of heat. The flame will pass through a piece of cloth without raising the temperature of the cloth. To obtain the same colored ray from steel a temperature of 2000° F. is required. By adding another element to the compound, the flame jumps to 3000° F.–3200° F. immediately. Hundreds of other examples might be given, corroborative of my experiments. I presume, however, as the foregoing are representative of all others, that they are all that is necessary. The most simple have been selected for the sake of the layman, who, as a rule, does not make a deep study of obtuse sciences.

It has been clearly shown that temperature does not in all cases govern the color of the ray. As I have shown, a white ray, which is generally understood to emanate from a superheated body only, also comes from cool bodies of atmospheric temperature. The actual factor governing the color of a ray, is the chemical compound of the body from which the ray emanates, and the difference, to a great extent, is due to the degree of radio-activity possessed by the substance emitting the ray.

As I have before stated, all bodies are more or less radioactive, although in nearly all, the degree is so low as to be unseen and unmeasurable. The cause for this general radio-activity is that the electro-magnetic division of the primary force permeates all substances, and, as a force is never still, but always moving, and as rays are the agents which move the forces, it can plainly be seen why all substances are radio-active.

I have previously stated that what is erroneously called solar or sun's heat is governed by the angle at which the sun's rays meet the earth's forces in the atmosphere. Herewith I give an illustration:

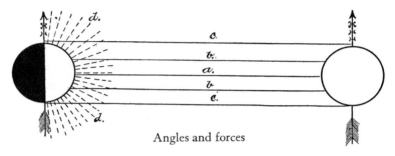

Angles and forces

Angles A^1 and A^2 show the sun's forces cutting the earth's lines of forces at the most obtuse angle from the sun, but at right angles of the lines of force. Angles B^1 and B^2 are obtuse, but not to the degree of Angles A^1 and A^2. The sun's forces cut the earth's lines of forces at an obtuse angle, so that to a certain extent the earth's lines are followed a distance by the sun's forces, giving a greater effect than when going through them at right angles.

Angle C. Here the sun's forces meet the earth's lines of forces end on, and work from end to end of the line, thus producing the maximum effect. The foregoing is proven from the fact that where the sun's forces cut the earth's lines of forces at right angles, we have our frigid zones; where the earth's lines are cut obtusely, we have our temperate zones;

and where the earth's lines are cut throughout their whole length, we see the maximum result — our tropical or torrid region.

My next illustration of angles and effects will be with a pair of armor plates undergoing ballastic test.

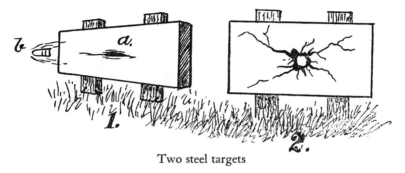

Two steel targets

These two targets are of equal strength and resisting power. One is placed so that it is at an obtuse angle to the gun, corresponding with the sun's rays when they are obtusely cutting the earth's lines of forces. The other target is placed at direct angles to the gun, like the sun's forces striking our torrid zones. The same gun is used, the same projectile is used, and the same charge for both. All conditions are the same except the angles at which the targets are placed with respect to the gun.

Fig. 1. The obtuse angle. On reaching the target, the projectile ploughs along its face a little, a—and then flies off at a tangent, b. The target is not penetrated.

Fig. 2. Right angles. The projectile passes clear through the target.

The difference in effect of these two shots is caused solely by angles; so it is with the sun's forces striking the earth's forces. The power and force are the same from pole to pole, the difference in effect—variations of temperature—is entirely due to the difference in the angles at which the sun's forces cut the earth's lines of forces. The four seasons, which are variations in temperature, are due to the oscillation of the earth's poles, which change the angle of the sun's rays.

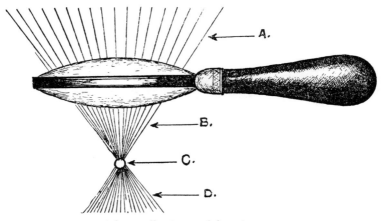

A lens collecting and focusing rays

Rays with their forces may be collected and concentrated and their effects magnified by the use of a lens. An ordinary lens is a piece of clear glass convexed on both sides. It has the faculty of collecting all of the rays that fall upon its face or upper surface and then concentrating or focusing them at a given point beyond the lower surface. The distance from the lens of the focus point is governed by the convexity of the glass.

I shall now describe an experiment with focused rays and the heat force.

The source will be a 100-candle power electric lamp. At the focus point the rays with their forces are drawn together and form an incandescent spot or point. This bright spot arises from an accumulation and concentration of the light force at the focus point. The accumulation is due to a number of rays, with their volumes of the light force, meeting and crossing each other in the area represented by the focus spot. This may be compared to a funnel subject to super-pressure.

At the focus point, the rays carrying the heat force are collected and concentrated like those of the light force. The heat thus concentrated is capable of burning up substances, and if the lens is large and powerful enough to melt platinum, the light rays may be veiled and repelled leaving only the heat rays to focus at the point. In this case there will be no incandescent spot, but the platinum will be melted all the same.

It may be claimed that the glass is in some way responsible for the super-heat. To prove that it is not, I shall make a lens out of a piece of ice and get the same results. As the ice does not melt, it shows that the heat force is carried in the rays passing through the ice, and in this condition it is a cold force.

I cannot do better at this point than to repeat certain experiments made by the late John Tyndall, experiments which I have duplicated many a time, and each time gained some knowledge about rays and forces.

As Cuvier was the father of paleontology, so Tyndall unknown to himself was the father of the science of forces. Tyndall never fully appreciated his own greatness.

Before taking extracts from his lecture and showing his experiments, I shall mention a few points about affinities and repellents, as they are very clearly shown in Tyndall's work.

AFFINITIES. An affinity may be either a force or an element, or an elementary compound, and is disclosed where one is seen to be attracted by the other,—when one is drawn towards the other. The magnetic needle is an example of an affinity between a force and an element.

REPELLENTS. A repellent may be either a force or an element, and is shown where one casts off the other.

NEUTRALS. A neutral may be a force or an element, and is shown where one has no influence over the other.

A magnetic force is an affinitive force when it attracts and draws towards itself.

A centrifugal force is a repellent force, as it throws off, casts away from itself.

The movements of bodies are accomplished by either affinitive or repellent forces, sometimes both.

Rays carrying forces have their affinities, repellents, and neutrals, in other rays and colors. Colors have their affinities, repellents, and neutrals in rays, also in colors.

EXTRACTS FROM JOHN TYNDALL'S LECTURE. "A common sunbeam contains rays of all kinds and colors but it is impossible to sift or filter out the beam so as to intercept all of the light rays, and allow the dark obscure ones to pass unimpeded; or, to filter out all of the dark rays and allow the light rays only to pass through, but for all practical purposes this can be done. Substances have been discovered which while extremely opaque to the light rays, are perfectly transparent to others. On the other hand, it is possible with the choice of proper substances to intercept to a great degree the pure heat rays[1] and to allow the pure light rays free transmission. This separation cannot be made as perfect as filtering the light rays. We have never seen the movements of waves that produce light, but we judge of their presence, their position, and their magnitude by their effect. Their lengths, however, have been determined and found to vary from 1/30,000th to 1/60,000th part of an inch.

---

1. Here Tyndall assumes that the ray is the force. I have hitherto pointed out that the ray is the carrier of the force and not the force itself.

"But besides the rays which produce light and heat, the sun sends forth multitudes of other rays. The largest and most powerful rays which the sun sends forth are of this character.[2]

"Heat issuing from any source not visibly red cannot be concentrated so as to produce the effects about to be referred to. To obtain this it is necessary to use a ray emanating from a body raised to the highest state of incandescence.[3]

"The sun is such a body, and its dark rays are therefore suitable for our experiments. But for such experiments as we are about to make, a little sun of our own is sufficient, an electric light. The electric light has also an advantage, as its dark radiation embraces a larger proportion of the total radiation of the sun's rays. An elecric light is therefore not only suitable, but best for the experiments we are about to make."[4]

EXPERIMENT I. "From the source of an electric light a powerful beam may be sent through the room, revealing in its passage the motes in the air, for, were there no motes, the beam would not be seen.[5]

"Let the beam fall on a concave mirror. It will be gathered up in the mirror into a cone of reflected light. The luminous apex of the cone is the focus point. Now place in the path of the beam a substance perfectly opaque to light. The substance to be used is iodine dissolved in a liquid bi-sulphate of carbon. The light at the focus point will immediately vanish when the

2. The sun's rays do not carry either the light or heat forces. These are both earthly forces. The most powerful rays and forces which the sun sends forth are those which control the movements of the bodies of the solar system. These are magnetic forces.
3. I have previously shown that bodies are not incandescent; the dark parent ray precludes the possibility of it.
4. At least one-half of the sun's dark radiation is unmeasurable on account of its intensity. This part of the sun's dark radiation is an extreme. Electric lamps also vary in their dark radiation, dependent on the elements forming the film.
5. The beam here spoken of by Tyndall is not the parent ray, it is a collection of rays of all colors, but separate from one another. They are the rays shown shooting off from the pyramidal zig-zag (Page 100). Dark rays do not disclose the motes in the atmosphere, only the light rays.

dark solution is introduced. But this dark solution is intensely transparent to the dark rays, and a focus point of these dark rays remains after the light has been abolished. The heat of these rays can be felt[6] by the hand. You can let them fall on a thermometer and thus prove their presence, or, best of all, you can cause them to produce a current of electricity which will affect a large magnetic needle.

"We shall now filter the dark rays so as to intercept the dark rays. This can be done with a clear solution of alum and water. It will permit the purely luminous rays to pass through. Place a small piece of gun cotton at the focus point and let the luminous rays exert their utmost power over it; no effect whatever is produced. Withdraw the alum filter and allow the full beam unfiltered to fall upon it. The cotton is immediately dissipated in an explosive flash. This proves that the light rays are incapable of exploding the cotton, while the rays of the full beam are competent to do so. Hence we might conclude that the dark rays are the real agents: but this conclusion might only be probably, for it might be argued that the mixture of the dark rays and the light rays is necessary to produce the result.

"Now by means of the opaque iodine solution let us filter the light rays and allow the dark rays to focus on the cotton, it will explode as before. Hence it is the dark rays and the dark rays alone that cause the ignition of the gun cotton. At the same focus point a sheet of platinum will become red-hot, zinc will melt, and paper will instantly blaze, and all the while the atmosphere around the focus point remains as cool as that in any other part of the room."

I cannot conceive of any experiment better than the foregoing to demonstrate and prove:

---

6. The rays cannot be felt. What is felt is the heat carried in them.

1. That there are parent rays, and that these parent rays are made up of a multitude of various colored rays.

2. That in our specialized atmosphere these parent rays are divided up and each separate ray filtered out and isolated from all the others.

3. That there are two prominent divisions coming out of the parent ray. One division is composed of light visible rays, the other of dark invisible ultra rays.

4. That the light rays carry the light force and do not carry a particle of the heat force.

5. That some of the dark rays carry the heat and magnetic forces, but not a particle of the light force.

6. That some colors are affinitive to the light rays, and these same colors are repellent to the dark rays.

7. That some colors are affinitive to the dark rays, and these same colors are repellent to the light rays.

8. That affinities partake of the same colors. Dark rays are affinitive to dark colors and light rays are affinitive to light colors.

On studying the foregoing experiment, it would seem that Tyndall only attempted to prove that there were two kinds of rays, light and dark; that the light rays were responsible for light and the dark rays responsible for heat and magnetism.

These points he most conclusively proved, but, he stopped short in his oratory—his experiments proved ten times as much as he pointed out and claimed.

I think Tyndall was under the impression that it was the rays themselves that were responsible for the various phenomena, and, indirectly, they were; but directly, it was the forces which were carried in the rays that were the direct agents. Tyndall omitted to show the difference between the rays and the forces they carried. He also omitted to explain why the different colored solutions or veilings were responsible for the different effects. He failed to point out affinities and repellents, which leads to the conclusion that he either overlooked them or was not aware of the facts.

This experiment demonstrates and proves out some of the characteristics of the workings of the forces. For instance: it shows that there are affinities and repellents in colors, for, when the rays from the electric lamp arrived at the dark solution, the color of the solution repelled the light rays, but permitted the dark rays to pass through, and as the heat remained at the focus point, it proves that the dark solution was extremely affinitive to the dark rays and their forces. This experiment also demonstrates and proves that the light solution was affinitive to the light rays and repellent to the dark ones.

It may be argued that the light solution did not repel the dark rays and their forces but absorbed them. If this were the case, there should be an accumulation and a concentration of the heat force in the light solution which should raise its temperature. I have duplicated this experiment several times, and not once did the temperature of the light solution rise a particle of a degree, thus convincingly showing that the dark rays with their forces were repelled, and not absorbed. Tyndall did not explain why an electric current should deflect the magnetic needle.

There were two separate and distinct rays that passed through the dark solution. One of the rays was an "ultra-steely" blue. This carried the magnetic force. The other was an ultra-red or reddish brown. This ray carried the heat force. It must be understood that when I mention two rays, I do not mean that they were all that passed through the filter. On the contrary, they were only two out of a multitude, but these two apply to the phenomena in question.

The iodine filter was affinitive to both the heat and the magnetic ray in question. It was more affinitive to the heat ray than to the magnetic ray. There was, however, a sufficient volume of the magnetic force concentrated to deflect the needle.

The needle was deflected because all forces coming out of the electro-magnetic division of the primary force have a tendency to join, aggregate, and concentrate. In this case it was an attempt of the concentration of the force in the focus point, to draw out that which was concentrated in the needle, thus making a greater aggregation. The magnitude of the deflection of the needle would indicate the size of the volume of the force aggregated and concentrated at the focus point. Tyndall's experiment shows that electricity, which is the main branch of the electro-magnetic division, can be subdivided into three separate sub-branches, namely, light, heat, and magnetism. In addition to these three, I have filtered out a dozen or more separate rays with their individual forces, and can truly say that this dozen does not represent the first letter in the alphabet of the whole tale.

To finish this section, and to corroborate Tyndall, I shall make a little experiment of my own, a simple natural phenomenon that can be understood by a child.

BLACK AND WHITE. The following are simple examples of affinities:

Place two pieces of iron on the ground, cover one with a white cloth, the other with a black. Let them be placed where the sun's rays fall directly on them. In an hour, measure the temperatures of the two pieces of iron. The one under the black cloth will be many degrees higher in temperature than the one under the white. Instead of two pieces of iron, take two cakes of ice. The one under the black cloth will be completely melted before the cake under the white cloth is half gone.

Suspend two pieces of cloth in the sun for an hour—one white and the other black. The black at the end of the hour will be many degrees hotter than the white. When a lady disbelieves that we do not get our heat from the sun and there is no such thing as affinities in colors, persuade her to put a white stocking on one leg with a white shoe on the foot and dress up the other leg and foot in a black stocking and shoe, then go out and sit in the sun where the rays strike directly on them. In a short time she'll be coming in to replace the black with white. This experiment may seem out of place here, but it is based on an actual test, and, believe the writer when he says there were no further proofs necessary to convince that lady.

The explanation of these phenomena is that black is an affinitive to the heat force, white a repellent.

All rays carry forces. Some rays have peculiar effects on human beings, brute animals, and plant life.

The force carried by a peculiar blue ray induces sleep and unconsciousness to pain. The force in a red ray induces a fighting spirit. There is much truth in the old saying, "like a red rag to a bull." Sunstroke is the effect of a certain ray striking the back of the neck and penetrating the cerebral cord. A red, vermilion, is the repellent of this ray. A red cloth falling over the back of the neck will prevent sunstroke. The force that causes sunstroke can no more pass through a piece of red cloth than the light rays could pass through John Tyndall's dark mixture.

[114]

SURGERY AND MEDICINE OF THE FUTURE. Forces are nature's tools for performing her works. All forces have opposites. One particular force will induce a growth, its exact opposite will kill it. The force may be known by the color or tint of the ray it is carried in. Therefore in the exact opposite colored ray will be found the counteracting force. This can be worked out in the form of a star with the three primary colors.

The science of medicine and surgery will, I feel sure, in the near future, be governed to a great extent by the use of forces through rays, rather than that of drug and knife. The time is ripe for this discovery to be made by the medical fraternity.

As no doubt the force will be known by the color of the ray by which it is carried, to avoid confusion and induce simplicity I shall speak of the force as being the ray, but it must be understood that I say most emphatically that the ray is not the force, only its carrier.

The physician and surgeon have to deal with the elementary part of the body—the machine itself. I have previously stated that forces have their affinitives, repellents, and neutrals in elements, thereby showing that the elements may be and are affected by the forces. Some forces will induce a growth, another force will kill it, and the third and neutral will not affect it in any way.

Each colored ray carries its own peculiar and definitive force. Rays again are dividable into tints, and each tint carries its own definite force.

All compounds of elements are subject to destruction from the application of some force. Therefore some ray bacteria, germs and growths such as cancer and tuberculosis, are all elementary compounds. Therefore they are all subject to destruction by the application of the right rays.

One particular ray may be found that will kill a germ and

yet not affect a growth and vice versa. It is only necessary to discover the right rays for each particular purpose.

Glass as filters should be avoided, as the tint is never uniform throughout the plate and no two plates are identically alike. Taking a piece of colored glass a foot long, one end may filter out one particular tint and the other end a different tint, and yet a third in the middle, each tint carrying a separate and distinct force. On this point I speak from experience, and yet the glass to all intents and purposes appears the same.

I know of no substance that is perfect, but it exists, and may be found by those who have the time, inclination, means and perseverance.

A FEVER. A fever is indicated by a rise in the temperature of the body. The rise is due to a super-amount of the vital life force in the body, and is the beginning of a step, which, if continued, will aggregate the force to such an extent that the force banked up and aggregated in the body will overbalance the elements. Then all movements and functions will cease. The life will pass away.

For a body to be normal, the force after having passed through the system in the form of Ziis, and become exhausted or tired out, should pass unobstructed from the body through the pores of the skin. Perspiration, which is water, is an exceedingly strong affinitive force. Perspiration attracts, collects, and carries off exhausted forces, thus leaving the channels open for following forces to take their place.

When perspiration ceases, or when the pores of the skin get clogged in any way, the exhausted forces have no exit, no means of escape. Then they bank up and clog all channels, eventually, if not relieved, back to the heart. Thus heat, one of the constituent parts of the life force, becomes accumulated in the body and raises its temperature.

During a fever, it will be noticed that the breathing of the patient is weak, short, and spasmodic, with a fluttering weakened heart action. This peculiar action of the heart is due to its inability to dispose of the forces brought to it by every breath through the lungs. The heart is trying to drive the force into channels already filled up.

The lungs, which are the channels of the force to the heart, have to be governed by the capabilities of reception by the heart—hence the short, weakened, spasmodic breathings. The heart, with all channels ahead blocked, can only accept from the lungs just what it can force into the filled channels. When it can force no more, then the next cannot be disposed of by the heart, the heart being incapable of handling it, breaks down and stops altogether—a phenomenon called by physicians "heart failure." The volume of the force taken in in breathing may be in excess of the central point of the range, on what physicians term "normal" without endangering life, provided the pores are kept open and action accelerated, i.e., perspiration accelerated and increased. The actual danger arising from a fever is not the question of temperature, but an overbalance of the elementary compound of the body.

A change in the volume of force also means the advent of new forms of life. As the temperature of the body ascends above normal, new forms of life are liable to appear within the body. The blood is the part of the body very intimately connected with the force—therefore in the blood we may look for possible developments. The blood is made up of corpuscles. To me, each corpuscle is a life in itself. Each corpuscle is chemically arranged to carry a certain volume of the force. By blocking the pores of the skin, the corpuscles cannot dispose of their exhausted forces; yet they have to take in more from the heart, resulting in the corpuscle becoming very much overcharged and increased in temperature. Now comes a question: Can any new life be formed in or between the corpuscles? This I cannot say, for I do not know. But, the natural result of a prolonged fever would be microscopical life of some sort forming in the blood. A microscopical examination of the blood under such conditions would probably answer the question. I simply offer this suggestion for the benefit of science. I have stated that the exhausted forces leave the body through the pores of the skin. A dark, invisible ray carries them. Although this ray is invisible to the human eye, yet it has a color. If our atmosphere were so specialized, or if the forces left the body in sufficient volume to cause incandescence of the atmosphere, like lightning, all human beings, and all breathing animals, would appear surrounded by a halo of light, similar to what is pictured as angels to children. This halo would vary in length in human beings, also at different times. People with a strong heart and lungs would have an extended halo, and those with weak heart and lungs a curtailed halo.

Certain forces advance, and also cause certain growths. A growth is the work of a positive force.

The negative force will retard and kill the growth. By the word growths I intend to include all forms of life from germs to mammals.

Any disease caused by germs can be killed by the use of the negative force.

All forms of life and growths are governed by forces. All forces are carried in and delivered by rays. A gun fires a shot, it is the shot which kills, not the gun. The ray carries the force but it is the force which does the work, not the ray. The ray is the carrier of the force. The ray is not the force any more than the pitcher is the water it is carrying.

Each colored ray, and even each tint of the ray, carries its own distinctive force, so that as there are innumerable tints, so there are innumerable forces. The negative force is carried in the opposite colored ray to that which carries the positive force.

The positive and negative forces can be determined by a star formed out of three primary colors.

A certain force may cause the growth and expansion of a cancer; the negative force will kill it.

A certain germ may grow and multiply under the influence of a certain force; its negative force will kill the germs.

Chapter V. The Life Force

IN THE ancient Naacal writings, one of the forces most prominently spoken of is called by them the life force—probably because it is instrumental in the creation and the carrying on of life. The same great theme is also a prominent part of the writings on the Mexican stone tablets recently found by William Niven from 4 to 6 miles northwest of Mexico City. The two sets of writings are so near alike in details that no question remains but that the origin of the both are the same.

The workings of the life force formed a very favorite theme among these ancients. The numeral 9 was assigned as the symbol of this force. The esoteric meaning was: "to revolve in circles and orbits."

They trace the life force down to its final divisions, workings and final disposition. There are two vignettes in the writings, a picture of the next division to the last, which is a

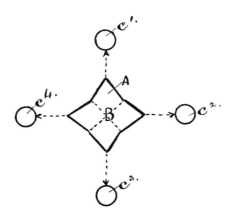

four-pointed star and corresponds with the electron of today. Another picture is the force in action. The four-pointed star has broken up into four globules or spheres. These attach themselves to the atoms and revolve them. As soon as they have completed their circle, they are exhausted and pass on, eventually being discharged through the pores of the skin.

THE LIFE OR VITAL FORCE. This is a vignette from the Naacal writings, a four-pointed star called Cahun. This word is composed of two vocables of the mother tongue: Ca means four and hun means one, therefore "four in one."

The probability is that the ancient interpretation of Cahun would be "dividable into four" or "divides into four."

The four-pointed star corresponds with the electron of today. It is the division of the life force next to the last one. This division is explained in the text. I have shown it by dotted lines through the center of the star.

After being broken up the divisions work into their ultimate shape as shown in C^{1234}. They are little revolving worlds in themselves.

In some drawings of the Naacals I find that these last divisions, these tiny revolving worlds, are not always drawn as perfect spheres, sometimes they are drawn as ovals. Whether this was intentional or not I cannot say. I found nothing about it in the writings.

These little revolving worlds are called Ziis. Neither the Zii or the Cahun can be seen by the human eye because they are forces, and being forces they are not apparent to vision. Their presence, however, is shown by the halo which they make in the atmosphere with their rays, like the film of an electric

light. The film itself is not seen; it is hidden within the halo it is casting. The eye sees the incandescence of the atmosphere only.

This figure is another Naacal vignette explaining the working of the Zii.

D. is the atom, or particle less than an atom.

C. are Ziis moving around the atom following one another as indicated by the arrows between each Zii.

In the text it is explained that the magnetic force of the Zii attaches it to the atom, causing the atom to revolve as shown by arrow D. After completing their circles carrying the atom around too, they pass on, but whether to another atom or out as an exhausted force I cannot say.

When the strength of the magnetic force in the Zii becomes exhausted, or becomes so low as to be inoperative, the whole Zii is carried off from the body through the pores of the skin. The whole Zii passes out, including the heat force which is associated with the magnetic in the Zii. Water is the great affinitive of the force, and in the form of perspiration becomes the transporting agent through the pores of the skin.

The life force is carried throughout the body by the blood. This figure is one of Niven's Mexican stone tablets, and is over 12,000 years old.

The glyph on this tablet reads Cahun. The same name as the Naacal. This glyph, however, has more than plain Cahun on it. It also says "under the guidance of the Creator's commands." The symbol of the Creator is of the Naga pattern.

In their spherical form, the last division, they are called Ziis. From the atmosphere they are drawn back with other exhausted forces to the central magnet; then they are regenerated and placed in the storehouse awaiting another call from nature.

The life force is a compound force, that is, it is composed of a number of distinct forces, starting as one combined force. It, however, separates and each one takes up its assigned duty. It is a sub-division of the electro-magnetic division. The Zii is one of these divisions in its final stage.

I have succeeded in partially dividing the life force, and have found that in it are (1) the heat force; (2) an elementary magnetic force, that is, elements drawing their kind to each other; (3) another magnetic combining force, that is, when elements are brought together this force combines them into one; and (4) a magnetic force out of which the Ziis emanate. Beyond this there are other forces which I have been unable to isolate.

One thing is certain, and can always be depended on. That is: the proportions of the various forces which go to make up the life force never vary, so that the volume of the life force may be computed by the reigning temperature, as the force heat constitutes one of the forces in the compound life force.

WHAT IS LIFE? Although perfectly understood by the scientists of the earth's first great civilization, life has always been one of the great mysteries of modern scientists. Since the time of the Brahmin usurpation of the Naacal temples about 2000 B.C., and later since the time of Darwin, who propounded the impossible theory of biological evolution, as an hypothesis, which he did not believe in himself, scientists have apparently devoted their time and energy to trying to discover the origin of species, and many a gaudy adornment has been pinned on to Darwin's hypothesis. Rather than exerting themselves in the direction of ascertaining the origin of species, why do they not try to find out the origin of life and what life is. These questions answered give also the origin of species.

Our scientists have been trying to build a castle in the air, a structure on a quicksand, a something without a foundation.

To discover the origin of anything it seems to me that we ought to go to the fountain head for it. Therefore, to satisfactorily determine the origin of species we must first know the origin of life itself. This is a foundation on which a structure can be built, and a structure that will stand.

Unfortunately, the bulk of scientists, since the time of Atlas, have been like a flock of sheep; the bell wether jumps the fence, then the whole flock follow him without rhyme or reason. All that the flock apparently aim at is to be thought orthodox.

Apparently, to them it does not matter how impossible, how silly, or how childish a theme may be, it is followed by the thousand simply to appear orthodox. What is the reason for this?

LIFE. As I see it, life is an elementary chemical compound brought together in certain percentages and proportions, one to the other, by an earthly force called by the ancients the life force.[1]

When all percentages and proportions, one to the other, of the elementary compound are correct, then a given volume of the life force balances the elements of the compound in such a manner that all parts, molecules, atoms and particles less than atoms, are started into movement, independently, and as a whole, like the wheels of a clock.

The movements at first are of a vibratory character, like the swinging of the pendulum of a clock, and when sufficient energy is attained it swings into a circular movement. This work is performed by the Ziis of the ancients. Ziis surround the atom, or particle less than the atom, circling around it and following one another. Their magnetic attraction to the element carries the element around on its axis.

Thus life consists of circular movements of elements. The

---

1. The whole life force is not involved in this step—only some of the forces in life's compound force, and these even may be disassociated from the others; that is, they may be independent.

power responsible for these movements is the life force. In using the word circular it is intended also to include orbits which may not be true circles.

After the circular movements are once started they are continued by the life force passing through the body like a weak electric current. The constant passage of the exact volume of the life force through the body keeps each and all parts and particles in regular and continuous movement.

To animate an elementary compound and to break it into life, requires a given volume of the life force to form the necessary balance. There is a short range in this volume, measured as temperature,—not more than 5° or 6° F. The range generally does not exceed 4° F. Hereafter I will give some examples.

When the volume of the force gets either above or below the range, the force becomes incapable of functioning. Then the life is blotted out. As an everyday example of the foregoing I will describe the hatching out of a hen's egg, which contains a life germ to be balanced by a given volume of the life force, to set its parts and particles into movement to form life.

The egg of the ordinary barnyard fowl will hatch out at a temperature of from 100° F. to 105° F. The ideal temperature, however, is 102½° F. This gives a perfect balance with the elements.

If, during the hatching period, the temperature of the egg is allowed to fall much below 100° F., the balance is upset, and movements stop. There is an insufficient volume of the force to balance the elements and keep them in movement. The force is overbalanced by the elements and the egg addles.

If the temperature is carried beyond 105° F. the elements are overbalanced, and movement ceases. The germ is killed.

[125]

Another instructive example is the hatching out of a nest of butterfly eggs. We will suppose that the perfect balance is 70° F. and the range is 5° F. I will now divide the nest into three parts, hatching out a part at 68½° F., a part at 70° F., and the balance at 72½° F.

Those hatched out at 72½° F. will be small and immature, those at 68½° F. full sized but dull in coloring, while those hatched out at 70° F., the perfect balance, will be full size, strong and vigorous, with brilliant colorings. The great difference in those hatched out at 68½° F. and 72½° F. is so marked, that one uniniated in insect life would believe that they were different species. This shows that at both ends of the range the life is not perfect. I shall show the cause of this hereafter in a section entitled specializations.

GROWTH. Provisions have been made by nature for replenishing worn out parts, and for adding new material to the elementary compounds forming the body, to increase size and to accomplish what is termed growth. In producing growth, two forces are especially active, the elementary magnetic and the combining forces. Food is supplied to these two forces to accomplish the work. The elementary magnetic force attracts, draws and measures out, from what has been taken in as food, the required material; and what is thus taken out must always be of the same elements as that which compose the compounds of the body, and that which is taken out is—always—in the exact proportions and ratio as the various compounds which go to form the body. No new element can be taken in without upsetting the vital balance. The combining force then carries this measured and selected material into chemical or intimate union with the various compounds forming the body, so that the original compounds are not chemically altered. They neither become more complex or more simple, so do not disturb the vital balance; if they did, the life would cease. I must emphasize the foregoing by repeating that all new material must always be in exact proportion or in the exact ratio that constitute the elementary compounds forming the body. This is so because an alteration in the original ratio upsets the balance with the life force, which would stop life's machine. This will be more fully explained in a section entitled: "Life's Machine."

When life comes either from the womb or ovum it is endowed with a given amount of instinct. This does not come from the elements forming the body, nor from the earthly forces animating it. It is one of the provisions made by the Creator, as a necessity for the continuance of the life. Man may, and can, with the aid of elements and forces, create life, but it remains with the Supreme Power to endow it with instinct and reason.

The foregoing is my foundation of life.

ORGANIC MATTER. It is without doubt appreciated by all scientists, and among most laymen that have given the subject a thought, that in the beginning there was no organic matter out of which life could be formed. For eons of time there was no life on this earth, because all was in a state called inorganic. It must also be appreciated that it was nature alone that changed matter from its inorganic state into organic. How was this done? Nature used her tools—her forces. What is organic matter? Organic matter is composed of elements out of which the seeds of life, cosmic eggs, may be formed.

In the beginning, as the earth's crust cooled from fusion, it was a single solid rock, too solid, and of too compact a character, from which to form the seeds of life.

The volcanic gases which had been placed in the granite rock and retained in the earth's center, broke asunder the outer

[127]

surfaces of the granite rock, and lifted them up, and crashed them down, over and over again. Through these liftings and crashing downs, the rocks were broken up and pulverized; oxidation, the work of an earthly force, followed, and was continuous on the surface rocks. These oxidations brought the elements down to a point, fine enough, where another earthly force was enabled to combine certain proportions of elementary matter into an intimate or chemical compound, when these elementary compounds were brought together, chemically joined, and in such proportions and percentages one to the other, also being capable of being balanced by a volume of the life force. Inorganic matter becomes not only organic matter, but also a seed of life, a cosmic egg.

In this manner nature formed her first life germs, seeds of life, out of which sprang life itself.

The life germ of today was the cosmic egg of the ancients of the earth's first great civilization.

LIFE GERMS. As previously stated, the earth's primary force permeates all earthly matter, also the atmosphere surrounding the earth. The life force is one of the sub-divisions of the primary force.

A life germ is an elementary compound and becomes a life germ in fact when the aggregation of the life force, held by the parts, molecules, atoms and particles less than atoms, balances the whole compound in such a manner that each and every particle, however infinitesimally small, breaks into movement.

I have used the word "aggregation" for the following reason: every part down to each particle of the elementary compound received its own individual volume of the force. The volume is dependent on the chemistry of the compound and various chemical compounds go to make up a living body.

Some elements and some elementary compounds are more affinitive to the force than others. These affinitive elements and compounds carry a relatively greater volume of the force than the less affinitive ones.

LIFE AS A MACHINE. Life is a machine, having many wheels fitting and meshing one into the other. Every atom and every particle of an atom of a living body represents a wheel in movement.

The volume of the life force which the atom or particle carries represents the size of the wheel.

The life force is the power which drives the machine and keeps the wheels turning.

The life force is taken from the air which we breathe. The air is permeated with it.

It is thus seen that, if in the compound one particular element is proportionately short or proportionately excessive, some wheels may become either too large or too small to mesh in with the next. Consequently in either condition the machine is out of order, and beyond a given point in shortage or excess the machine will stop. Hence my previous saying:

"Certain parts and percentages one to the other."

The bodies of all forms of life are composed of many different chemical elementary compounds, but all so arranged by nature's chemistry that each one is balanced by the volume of the life force present.

In parts of the body where powerful and rapid action is going on, it will be found that the chemical composition of these parts is very simple. The more simple the compound the more affinitive it is to the force; and, as the compound becomes more complex, so its affinity for the force proportionately drops. Thus nature provides for supplying heavily working parts with extra power.

[129]

As an example, certain glandular secretions are exceedingly affinitive to the force. These secretions are carried to their field of work by the blood to excite the cells into greater activity.

Scientists assert that certain glandular secretions are the actual agents which excite the cells. They are not the actual agents, they are only the carriers of the agent. The actual agent is the life force which in these compounds is carried in greater volume than in the less affinitive compounds.

THE ORIGIN OF SPECIES. The origin of species and their forms may be taken collectively, as they originate at the same time, through a change in elementary compounds.

It is a phenomena that the more simple an elementary compound is, the greater will be the volume of the life force necessary to balance it. As the elementary compound becomes more complex, so the volume of the life force must be proportionately lowered to balance it.

If the life germ is too complex for the volume of the force present, the elements are overbalanced and cannot break into life.

The shape and character of a life is governed by the component parts of the elementary compound forming the germ from which the life sprang, combined with the proportions of the elements one to the other.

A simple elementary compound is the mother of a simple form of life, and a complex form of life comes out of a complex compound. The life partakes of the character of its elementary compounds.

THE HOUSE OF LIFE. Life has been built up gradually, step by step, like the building of a house, brick by brick. The foundation stones of the house of life were tiny, microscopical marine grasses and lichens. The ancient writings of man constantly reminds the reader that "the waters were the mother of life"; that is, animal life first appeared in the waters.

For a time this minute marine vegetation composed the only forms of life on earth. When conditions became sufficiently advanced, which occurred when the volume of force present was sufficiently lower, by the earth's cooling, these first forms of life died down and decomposed, and out of their decaying bodies new life germs were formed. The new germs were not composed entirely out of the material of the decomposing bodies, only the major part; for, certain parts and percentages of other elements from surrounding substances were drawn into the forming germ which made a new and more complex germ.

In some cases entirely new elements were drawn in. In others only a rearrangement of the old elements was made, but in all cases the new germ was chemically more complex than the old life from which it emerged.

The new germ could not break into life until the volume of the force was lowered by the earth's cooling to a point where the force could balance the more complex germ, and break it into life.

The reason for the elementary changes in the compound of the new life germ was not in the elements themselves. It is well known to chemists that certain elements will only go into intimate or chemical union with other elements at certain temperatures, which means that they will only go into union by a given volume of the elementary combining magnetic force.

As time went on, the cooling of the earth gradually lowered the volume of the force present, which brought new and more complex germs, out of which sprang new and more complex lives. These new germs formed new lives and the new lives were new creations.

The life force has been gradually and regularly lowered in volume, both in the atmosphere and the earth during and throughout the cooling of the earth's crust. The lowering of the volume of the force has been in ratio with the earth's cooling, and became finally settled when the earth went into final magnetic balance, which occurred at the end of the tertiary era.

The lowered volume of the life force which balanced the new life germ became too low in volume to balance the compounds of the life which the new germ came out of. So the old life died out.

The old life did not evolve into the new life; the new life was a new creation to take the place of the old life. I have previously mentioned that the life force has a range, a very short one; that in this range there is a point where the balance between the elements and force is perfect, generally about the middle of the range.

If a balance exists which is above the perfect, the machine has too much power on; the movements of parts are too rapid for perfect development, resulting in dwarfed, spindly immature forms.

If a balance exists which is below the perfect, the machine has not sufficient power to work it perfectly; consequently the movements of the parts are too slow for perfect development, resulting in the irregular forms called by scientists specializations.

If the additions or changes, or both, be identically the same in two germs, coming out of the same body, the two new lives will be identically the same. If, however, the changes or additions, or both, vary in the two new germs, let us say from vegetation, it is within the range of possibilities that one of the germs might result in bringing forth a member of the vegetable kingdom, while the other might give life to a member of the animal kingdom—a protozoan of the lowest order, a mere cell.

The production of animal life, coming out of germs from vegetation, depends entirely on alterations in the relative percentages of the old compounds and new additional elements; for without these additions of new elements, the life would continue on in the vegetable kingdom.

As the shape and character of a life is governed by the compositions and arrangements of its elementary compounds, and as all creations come out of previous ones, and the major part of the germ comes from an old life, the new life must necessarily very strongly resemble and partake of the character of the one that went before it, and, to a certain extent, be representative of it.

This close relationship has been shown by the lives which have followed one another from the beginning of life upon the earth.

From the time of the early creations of life down to present time, both animals and plants as they succeeded one another have been so nearly alike in appearance, anatomy and character, that it becomes less than a wonder that the theory of evolution sprang out of it. Especially when our scientists know nothing about the life force, which was the factor in bringing about these changes.

There has, however, always been one great difference in each succeeding form of life. That difference has been that each succeeding form of life has been more complex than the preceding one.

That the new life did not come into existence contemporary with the old life is due to the fact that the elementary chemical compounds forming the new life were more complex than the old life and therefore required a lower volume of the life force to balance it; and this lower volume of force was below that required to balance the old life.

As the cooling of the earth from the beginning down to the end of the tertiary era was slow, gradual, and even, without a backward movement, and as the life force can be measured by temperature, it is thus seen that from the beginning the life force (like the surface temperature of the earth) has been lowering in ratio with the temperature. This clearly shows us that:

It was imperative that each succeeding life should be more complex than its predecessor; for, had not each succeeding life been more complex than its predecessor, the lowered force would not have balanced it, and no new life would have resulted. Thus, first life would have come into existence, then died out with the change in the volume of the life force, leaving the earth lifeless once more.

Apparent evolution of both animal and plant life are therefore only natural, for the reasons which I have pointed out, and the same reasons show that evolution is apparent only and not real.

A New Form of Life is a new building, in which many parts of an old building have been used. The old building has been torn down, it exists no longer; but the old doors, gables and windows have been used in the new structure, which gives it somewhat the appearance of the old.

A life starts small and primitive in form, because it comes into existence at the top of the vital range where the force slightly overbalances the elements. When the force has sufficiently lowered to effect a perfect balance, then food, environment and conditions carry the life to its zenith.

The Creation of a New Life. To create a new form of

life more complex than existing forms, it is imperative that the life germ from which the new life is formed shall come out of the dead remains of a previous life. Otherwise, the germ would be less complex, and incapable of being balanced by a lower volume of the force, and, being less complex, it would be a retrograde step in creation.

Quoting the biblical symbolical explanation, which I have found to have originated in the Motherland of Man more than 50,000 years ago: to create a woman it was necessary that the rib of man be taken from him during his sleep (the ancient name of death).

The ancients had no word corresponding with our word death. What we call death they called sleep. With them it was simply the sleeping of the soul until called upon to enter another house of clay to complete its allotted task: "attain perfection of the soul over the flesh." This is a virtual translation from one of the old Naacal writings.

This foregoing is confirmed by Niven's Mexican stone tablet No. 1584, Creation of Woman.

This tablet shows the working of the forces in the creation of the first pair, man and woman. The description of what life is, is vividly given in the Naacal writings. A full translation of it will appear in my work entitled "Life."

EVOLUTION IMPOSSIBLE. Evolution as applied to the origin of species is simply and utterly impossible, for it is utterly impossible to make a living animal chemically more complex, for the following reason: A chemical change in the elementary compounds of a living body upsets the vital balance. When the vital balance is upset, the machine is compelled to stop working, because one or more of the wheels in life's machine has been made either too large or too small to mesh in with the next wheel, or surrounding ones. In other words, in popular language: poison has been administered.

Death by poisoning is simply the result of adding to and changing some of the elementary compounds of the body, throwing it out of vital balance. Biological evolution, as being taught today, asserts that chemical changes take place in living animals, making them more complex. I have shown that this is absolutely impossible, because:

A chemical change means poison,
Poison means death, and
Death means the elimination of the life.
The life has disappeared forever.

Chapter VI. Specialization

I WILL now give some examples of the workings of the life force, taking first specializations, as these show the consistent workings of the force all through life, from the first land animals down to the end of the tertiary era.

Specializations are nature's great object lessons in showing the workings of the life force.

A specialization is shown by some extraordinary growth or development, something abnormal in a part or parts of the body. These specializations, sometimes amounting to fantastic forms of life, mark the beginning of the end of the crop in which they appear. The rapidity of the decline is governed by the life force as represented by temperature.

Towards the end of all crops both animal and vegetable, specialized, fantastic, gnarled forms are liable to appear, taking the place of previous perfect and symmetrical forms. Scientists call these "high specializations," which is a correct term; but, while they state what the phenomenon is, they fail to state or explain the cause. Some reckless scientists have gone as far as to call these "high specializations" steps in evolution; which is, as I have heretofore pointed out, perfect nonsense.

Specializations are nature's guideposts pointing out the fact that the crop is nearing its end, and that the end is due to the lowering of the life force.

As before stated, there is a range within which life will start and continue. In the case of specializations the force has fallen below the perfect balance. It is therefore insufficient to supply each and every part and compound with the requirements to keep all parts of the machine working in perfect unison. As I have stated, some elements have a greater affinity for the force than others. The glandular secretions are the most affinitive, and these also vary in affinity to a marked degree. With every breath a volume of the life force is taken into the body. The glandular secretions being the most affinitive, and the supply of force being short, these secretions obtain more than their fair share. Then, added to this, the most affinitive secretions get more than their proportion; the distribution of the force is therefore completely thrown out of gear.

It is attested by scientists that each glandular secretion performs certain special work of its own; so that the work which is done by those secretions results in some cases in its being done in full, in others only partially, and this results in overgrowth of some parts and shrinkage in others. The overgrowth on the one hand, and shrinkage on the other, produce the effect called specializations.

I think a little geology at this point, as an object lesson, will not be out of place. As this lesson I will discuss

THE RISE AND FALL OF THE GREAT REPTILES

Scene: Carbonic Era—An endless Swamp.
The Mastodonosaurus—Carbonic Amphibian.
The Dimetrodon—Carbonic Reptile.
Scene—Jurassic Period. A Swamp.
The Stegosaurus—Jurassic Reptile.
Scene: Early Cretaceous—Land less soft.
The Triceratops—Late Cretaceous Reptile.
The Trachodont—Late Cretaceous Reptile.
Scene: Early Tertiary—Swamps turned to marshes.

TYPICAL LAND DURING THE CARBONIC ERA. AN ENDLESS SWAMP

THE CARBONIC (PERMIAN) AMPHIBIAN MASTODONOSAURUS. HIGH SPECIALIZATION

SHOWN BY HEAD, MOUTH AND TEETH

This model was made especially for this work by Dr. C. W. Gilmore, Curator of Vertebrates, National Museum, Washington, D. C.

THE CARBONIC (PERMIAN) REPTILE DIMETRODON. EXTREME SPECIALIZATION, ITS ENORMOUS DORSAL FIN.

THE END OF A LONG ANCESTRY

[141]

AT THE END OF THE JURASSIC PERIOD WHEN THE GREAT REPTILES WERE AT THEIR PEAK. LAND, SWAMPS WITH DEEPER WATER THAN THE OLD SWAMPS OF THE CARBONIC—TEMPERATURE SUPER-TROPICAL

This model was made especially for this work by Dr. C. W. Gilmore, Curator of Vertebrates, National Museum, Washington, D. C. STEGOSAURUS, ONE OF THE MOST HIGHLY SPECIALIZED REPTILES OF THE JURASSIC PERIOD. ITS SPECIALIZATION IS ITS DORSAL PLATES

TYPICAL LAND DURING THE EARLY CRETACEOUS, WHEN THE GREAT SAUROPODS DIED OUT AND NEW FORMS TOOK
THEIR PLACE. MANY SWAMPS TURNED TO MARSHES. TEMPERATURE SUPER-TROPICAL

FIG. 1

FIG. 2

These models were made especially for this work by Dr. C. W. Gilmore, Curator of Vertebrates, National Museum, Washington, D. C.

FIG. 1—THE TRICERATOPS AT ITS ZENITH. FIG. 2—SPECIALIZATION SHOWN BY ITS GNARLED HEAD. READY FOR ITS GRAVE AND THE END OF THE GREAT REPTILES

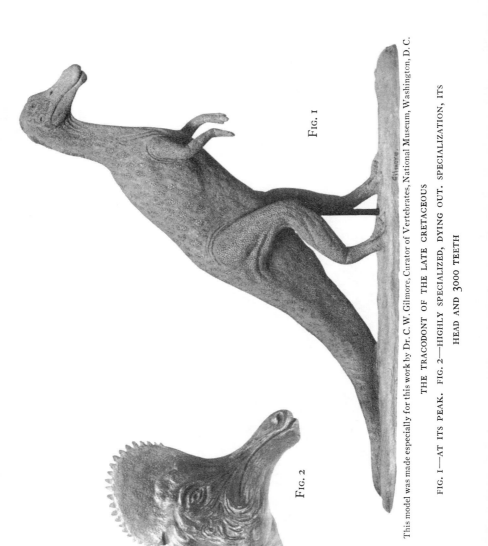

This model was made especially for this work by Dr. C. W. Gilmore, Curator of Vertebrates, National Museum, Washington, D. C.

THE TRACODONT OF THE LATE CRETACEOUS

FIG. 1—AT ITS PEAK. FIG. 2—HIGHLY SPECIALIZED, DYING OUT. SPECIALIZATION, ITS

HEAD AND 3000 TEETH

FIG. 1

FIG. 2

EARLY TERTIARY. LAND TURNED FROM SWAMPS INTO MARSHES, GENERALLY VERY SOFT, THE
ANIMALS HAVE LONG, SPREADING, WADING-BIRD-LIKE TOES

THE HORSE, A SPECIMEN OF THE EARLY TERTIARY ANIMALS, WITH ITS LONG, SPREADING, WADING-BIRD-LIKE FEET AND TOES

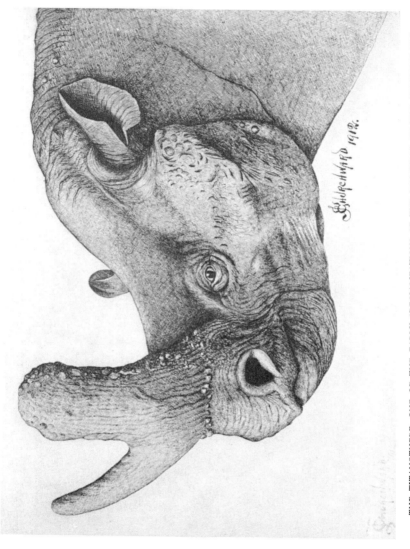

THE TITANOTHERE, ONE OF THE EARLY SPECIALIZATIONS OF THE MAMMALS OF THE TERTIARY ERA. IT DIED OUT DURING THE OLIGOCENE. ITS SPECIALIZATION IS SHOWN BY ITS HORN

THE SABRE-TOOTH TIGER, ONE OF THE LAST GREAT SPECIALIZATIONS OF THE TERTIARY MAMMAL LIFE.
LATE TERTIARY. ITS SPECIALIZATION IS SHOWN BY ITS TUSKS

Scene: Four-toed Horse—Mammal.
Titanothere—Tertiary Mammal.
Saber-toothed Tiger.

THE GREAT REPTILES. Geological records show us that the bones of the first known reptiles were found in the rocks of the carbonic era, prominently during the permian period. Some of those found in the permian rocks are exceedingly highly specialized, showing that they were the fag ends of a long ancestry; so that, to get back to the beginning of reptiles, we must go back beyond the permian period. How far back? That I cannot say, but I can say that from the beginning of life, the character and form of life was governed by a condition.

The condition for the advent of amphibian and reptile life was fully completed before the geological devonian era commenced, for this era commenced with the condition perfected.

Throughout the earth's development, commencing with the beginning of life, it has been clearly shown that suitable forms of life always accompanied the making of a new condition.

By the time the devonian era had arrived, the temperature of the earth, as shown by the luxuriant vegetation (with the life force having dropped to a point where it would balance a more complex elementary compound than that of fishes), new types of life came into existence, consisting of amphibians and reptiles. This has geologically been called the mesozoic or middle life.

Some of the carbonic permian amphibians and reptiles show very extreme specializations. Their forms have become fantastic in appearance, such as the great amphibian mastodonosaurus (see page 140) and the extraordinary reptiles

[151]

dimetrodon (see page 141), the naosaurus and other fin-back reptiles.

Great specializations appear in the permian armored variety of reptiles.

These specializations denote one thing, and one thing especially; that is: that the types of these animals were nearing their end; that they were not the first of their race,—they were the dying ends of an immensely long ancestry.

Specializations are the result of a changing condition, and as it takes an immensely long time to change a condition and to establish a new one, it is clearly seen that untold ages had elapsed between the first small primitive reptile and the huge, grotesque, highly specialized ones of the permian period.

Throughout the reptilian era, even with the meager knowledge which has been supplied to us by the rocks, it is very marked that the types of the great reptiles were changed from time to time, not suddenly, but rather in single rotation. First one form died out. Another was created to take its place. Then another died out, and again another took its place. And so it continued on until not a single form remained that had lived during a previous period of time. This complete change in the type and forms of life showed that a complete change in conditions had been made.

Reptiles reached their zenith during the jurassic period. This was the time of their greatest expansion. They grew to larger sizes and in greater numbers than at any other period in the great reptilian era.

When thus at their zenith, the cretaceous period commenced and the great jurassic reptilian expansion passed into the cretaceous.

The gradual and constant dying out of the various types of reptilian life, and the gradual appearance of new forms taking their place, corresponded with the gradual lowering of the earth's temperatures, and with it the gradual lowering of the volume of the life force.

Some forms were externally modified from time to time, until they could stand no further modifications; then these forms died out; their career had ended; they became lives of the past.

Following the carbonic era and during the jurassic, the life force became low enough to balance still more complex elementary compounds. Then the lowest types of life that were higher than reptiles began to appear; but, generally speaking, the life force during the jurassic and early cretaceous was too high in volume to balance any other animal compound beyond amphibians and reptiles.

The Carbonic reptiles could not live and reproduce during the Jurrassic because the force had fallen below the point or range of the carbonic compounds. Neither could the jurassic animals have lived during the carbonic era because the force was above the range of their compounds. In line with the foregoing it is noteworthy that as we leave our temperate zone and pass into the tropics, the animals which are found in the jurassic rocks of the temperate zone appear in the lower cretaceous in the tropics, which is of much later date than the jurassic. There are several records of this phenomenon.

THE CRETACEOUS PERIOD. During the Cretaceous Period, what is now the temperate part of North America dropped from a super-tropical down to a warm temperate with winters.

The low temperature is shown by the vegetation of the late Cretaceous Period.

About the end of the middle cretaceous and the beginning of the late Cretaceous, great changes took place in the reptilian life. Not a single form was handed down from the jurassic, and very few types remained.

A few new types appeared during the Cretaceous, and those coming down from the early Cretaceous were all becoming more and more specalized. Many assumed grotesque and fantastic forms. The lowering of the life force was responsible for it.

The highly specialized form of the triceratops (see page 145) and the trachodonts (see page 146) should cause no astonishment to scientists. They were the result of a never-failing natural law. By their great specializations they showed that the great reptiles were near their end; they were standing on the brink of their graves.

The peculiar phenomenon of fantastic, gnarled, irregular or specialized forms appearing in a disappearing crop, does not relate to animal life alone. It permeates all forms of life, including fish and vegetable. Nature is constantly illustrating this to us. We have only to walk through a garden in the fall, when the temperature has dropped from a summer heat and the life force with it, to see this law being carried out wherever we look.

The last few apples on the topmost branches of the tree are small, gnarled and irregular. The last few roses on the bush are small, lopsided and irregular. The last few tomatoes on the vine are gnarled, small and of irregular shape, and so on throughout the garden. All denoting that the life force is below their perfect balance. Either the temperature of the cretaceous period was guilty of a sudden drop or the cretaceous period was ten times as long as assigned to it by geology.

I do not base the length of the Cretaceous Period on the rock formation of the time, because many rocks which geology says took hundreds of thousands of years to form were, as a matter of fact, formed in a few days.

Following one of the great natural laws, the earth's cooling has been even, slow, regular and methodical. It is self-evident from the lessons given by its vegetation and animal life that the cretaceous period was not guilty of irregularities in cooling. There was no sudden drop in temperature. Therefore the cretaceous can boast of having covered an immensely long period of time. All forms, classes and types of life, animal, bird, fishes and vegetation, convincingly show that the earth's temperatures dropped more during the Cretaceous Period than they did all through the long geological Paleozoic Time.

During the Cretaceous Period the temperature of temperate North America dropped from super-tropical down to a warm temperate. A ten times greater drop than from the Cretaceous down to today, and a greater drop than was made from the first Cambrian rock down to the last Carbonic stone.

At the beginning of the Cretaceous the vegetation was all of a super-tropical swamp growth. At the end of the Cretaceous it was mostly of a hard ground growth, with the trees showing wintering rings.

I have pointed out great specializations and the dying out of the great reptilian race. Why did these forms die out? This is a question geology does not attempt to answer. I think I have, and correctly, too.

It is no wonder that the great, coarse, ungainly, fierce, cruel and terrible mesozoic monstrosities died out, in apparently a very sudden manner, for the volume of the life force became too low to hatch out their eggs. Nature imposed the penalty, and carried it out in its own manner, for disposing of the coarse, imperfect mesozoic life. They had been rank weeds in the garden and were doomed to be rooted out. With the passing of the Cretaceous, the earth was forever rid of the monstrous mesozoic life.

FACTS VERSUS THEORY. Many of my friends have requested that I include a chapter in this work on the all-absorbing theory of biological evolution.

Theory is always subservient to facts.

In the previous chapter I have, I think, reasonably and I trust satisfactorily, shown that evolution such as is being preached and taught today, is impossible, because the various forms of life which have succeeded one another have been governed by the vital life force, and this force has called for a more complex form to succeed its predecessor; and that while this force is bringing forward a new life, it is killing off the old.

In this chapter I can only show the errors which are prominent in the theory of evolution, by bringing forward certain phenomena and facts, showing that what has been termed steps in evolution has been mere physical modifications, made in the animals to suit them to their environment and surrounding conditions. These changes have been mere modifications without in any way making the animal either more complex or more simple.

For fifty years scientists all over the world have been vainly hunting for the "missing link," the link that connects man with monkeys. Being unable to find this, they gave up the search. Now they are off on another hunt. They are looking and hunting for that which was forefather to both man and monkey. What sort of beast they expect to find I cannot imagine. I think I have scientifically and to all reasoning and reasonable minds, proved that evolution is impossible and have shown how the phenomena occurred upon which the theory of evolution has been built up.

Even our dictionaries have caught the taint. On consulting a prominent one, I find: "Evolution is a succession of changes by which a body passes into a more complex form." I have shown that to change a body into a more complex form the vital balance is upset and the body dies, because the machinery of life is stopped. The body has been poisoned.

To sustain the theory of evolution, a scientist writes: "Besides the main line of descent which led to the modern horse, ass, and zebra."

It is here distinctly asserted that the horse, ass, and zebra descended from a common forefather. Today they are chemically different from one another, so that this assertion carries with it the idea that these chemical changes were made during the lives of the animals since the Eocene Time, which is impossible for reasons heretofore stated.

The horse, the ass, and the zebra did not descend from a common forefather. They are today and always have been separate and distinct animals. Each of their first ancestors was chemically different, and this chemical difference has continued down to present time and will continue as long as the animals exist.

I have made a very emphatic statement. Some evolutionists may ask: Where are your proofs? I would not have made the statement without being prepared to uphold it with reasonable proofs. I shall bring forward a trilogy of proofs: chemistry, natural laws, and the workings of the forces.

When animal life was first started by the Great Creator, natural laws for its continuance were laid down. These laws have been most implicitly followed from the beginning, and are in full force today. One of the great natural laws concerning life is this: there shall be no confusion of species. This natural law was so well known and appreciated by the ancients that it became embodied in the Levitical law. The penalty imposed by nature for an attempt to introduce confusion of species was, and is today, barrenness to the first product; so that confusion of species never could, and cannot today, be continued. As the first product cannot reproduce, the confusion begins and ends with the first.

To change the species of an animal, or to make it more complex, internal chemical changes must be made. First a chemical change must be made in the elementary compounds of the body, not any one or two parts, but the whole. This is poison and means death. Chemical changes must be made in the generative secretions, and the feeding fluids for them, with which to continue life, after the germ is once animated. To change one part of the elementary body without changing the whole, would be to put a big wheel in life's machine where a small one belongs, or vice versa.

While nature permits of external modifications that do not affect the elementary compounds of the body, it absolutely forbids internal changes which do affect the elementary compounds of the body and consequently the vital balance.

When two separate species of animals are crossed, the product is what is termed a mule. A mule is barren and cannot reproduce. This is so on account of internal changes. In crossing, two separate and distinct elementary compounds have been mixed together, resulting in throwing certain parts of the dual compound out of balance with the vital force. These parts are the generative organs and the generative secretions.

If a new and more complex animal could be born or evolved from a more simple one, there is no reason why specimens of each form should not be found contemporary with each other. One where the change has been made, the other before it was made. Have ever these two specimens been found together? Contemporary with each other? It would seem to be impossible that millions of a species should make a date for a general change, and then all keep it without a single laggard left behind.

If the elementary compound of the simple animal was in balance with the vital force, and the elementary compounds of the more complex animal was also in balance with the force, then there is no reason why some of the gigantic reptiles of the mesozoic time should not be found in the endless swamps of South America and Africa; or when we go a-fishing, trouble might be met in bringing an obstreperous ichthyosaurus or a pugnacious tyrolosaurus to the gaff—and one might look forward to quite a long-reach fight with the elasmosauraus.

When an evolutionist is asked why none of these old forms are not still with us, his answer is, "Some died out, the others evolved into our present animals." Yet no real connecting link has ever been found between fishes and amphibians, amphibians and reptiles, reptiles and mammals, or monkeys and men. By a great stretch of imagination, there are a few cases where succeeding forms have a great resemblance to one another, and to the preceding ones; so that, if one did not know it to be impossible, he might come to the conclusion that one was born of the other, with external modifications made to suit surroundings and environment. Yet, in these cases even, a close analysis invariably shows marked differences. During the late Cretaceous Period, the earth was infested with huge terrible reptiles, such as the Tyramnosaurus, Trachodonts, and Triceratops. At the commencement of the Eocene Period, the beginning of the Tertiary Era, we find the earth is peopled with little mammals about the size of dogs and foxes. The Eocene followed directly after the Cretaceous. The first Eocene formation rests on the last of the Cretaceous.

It is a well-known fact among geologists that there is a long period of time between the last Cretaceous and the first Tertiary in most rock formations. Thus there is a corresponding break in the continuity of life, so that the development of life during this period has not been traced. Nature, however, always supplies an object lesson somewhere, if we will only look for it, and appreciate it when we find it. This lesson which has been withheld in most rock formations is to be found in Venezuela, South America.

Dr. Siever, a German scientist and traveller, found in the mountains of northern Venezuela a limestone which he called the "Capacho Limestone." In it he found fossils "of the higher chalk formation" (Upper Cretaceous).

Upon this foundation he found other strata which he has called "the Cerro de Cro series or Golden Hill," on account of the great quantity of iron pyrites found there. These rocks fill in the time between the last geological Cretaceous and the first Tertiary, Eocene rock.

Dr. Siever says: "There was a continuous series of deposits, so that we have at the base chalk fossils and higher up eocene forms. The general character of the animal life—changing gradually from one to the other." From reptiles to mammals.

Geologically speaking, this great change occurred over night. Here is the great dividing line between ancient and modern forms of life. At this line should be found examples of evolution if evolution is a fact. Have any ever been found? Before the theory of evolution is advocated or advanced, the advocate of it should be prepared to point out some of the changes being made from reptilian to mammal life. For, here at this line was made the most radical step in animal life that has been made during the whole development of the animal life on earth. He should point out the eocene descendants of the tyrannosaurus, triceratops, and the trachodonts. He should be able to point out the reptilian forefathers of the tiny eocene

[160]

mammals, and he should have a reasonable reason for the tremendous shrinkage in size of the eocene life compared to the life of the late Cretaceous.

The cretaceous dinosaurs reared their heads above the ground from 15 to 25 feet. The eocene animals, generally, were less than two feet at the shoulder. The answering of the foregoing questions should be easy to the evolutionist, as the change, as before stated, geologically speaking, "was made over night." Can the evolutionist show a single case where one animal is changing into another such as the missing link between a reptile and a mammal?

Now I shall take up the question of modifications made by nature to suit the animal to its environment, which scientists have claimed to be steps in evolution. Modifications are not only permitted by the great natural law, but nature herself assists in making the necessary modifications. These modifications are always external only and do not in any way effect the elementary compounds of the animal or its internal arrangements. They in no way simplify the animal or make it more complex. Examples of modifications are:

An extra development of a part or a member.
A lengthening or shortening of the limbs.
Changes in the shape and character of the foot.
Changes in the character of the covering.
Changes in coloration.

I shall now point out some of these examples in past and present life. The shape and character of the feet of an animal are a certain indication of the character of the ground over which it habitually roams and feeds. Animals such as our present-day caribou, which habitually selects soft, marshy ground on which to live, have enormous pan-like hoofs. When this animal, which is the same as the reindeer of Europe, is kept and bred on hard dry ground, its feet with each generation become smaller and smaller until finally they are characteristic of all the deer family.

The wild cattle of the Dismal Swamp of Virginia have large pan-like hoofs characteristic of the caribou, yet these cattle are the descendants of ordinary cattle which, long ago, strayed into the swamp and were lost. Their feet became modified to suit the ground of the swamp.

The animals of the Eocene Period were all very remarkable for their long spreading toes, typical of our present-day wading birds, which frequent the soft, muddy, marshy shores of ponds, lakes, and streams. The feet of the eocene animals thus clearly show the character of the ground during the eocene period. Their feet were adapted for carrying their owners over soft, muddy, marshy, spongy ground. In my geological work I have shown that the ground of the Eocene Period was of this soft character and gave the causes and reasons why it was so. Among the Pueblo Indian traditions there is a very vivid and amusing description of the character of the ground at this period. This tradition I gave in "The Lost Continent of Mu."

I shall now take the little eocene horse with its long wading-bird-like feet to show the relative modifications, because the eocene horse has been one of the principal examples used to uphold evolution.

It is geologically stated that the eocene horse commenced life with five long wading-bird-like spreading toes on each foot. These, when spread out, prevented the weight of his little body from sinking his feet and legs into the soft ground over which he habitually travelled. Had he not been thus properly provided for by nature for rapid travel over soft ground, his feet would have sunk into the soft marshy ground. Then his pace, his only defence against his enemies, would have been retarded, and he would have fallen an easy prey to some carnivorous animal which was better provided for travel over soft ground. As the ground drained out and hardened during the following Oligocene, Miocene, and Pliocene Periods, we see that kindly nature was ever looking after the little fellow's welfare by modifying his feet to suit the ever-hardening ground, so that his great speed was always maintained. During the greater part of the Miocene and the whole of the Pliocene, long soft toes, such as he had during the Eocene, would have been totally unsuited to the ground. His toes would have been cut and maimed by the sharp stones when galloping over them. So nature attended to the necessary changes to suit the condition of the times. The horse's feet today are in the best possible shape for rapid travel over hard ground, so that he is enabled to out-distance his enemies when pursued by them.

The theory of evolution is that an animal becomes more complex during life, and the advocates of this theory have referred to the horse as an example, claiming that the changes in its feet were steps in evolution. In the first place, no actual changes have been made in the horse's foot from the Eocene time down to the present day. Modifications only have been made. All the changes that have been made in the horse's foot from the Eocene down to the Pliocene did not make him either more complex or more simple, and, his elementary compounds have never been changed. As before stated, what really happened to him was simply a modification of shape by the extra development of a member and the shrinkage of other members. Yet scientists claim that these mere modifications are steps in evolution. If they were steps in evolution, the horse of today would be more complex than the horse of the Eocene

[163]

time. As the horse of today is not more complex than the eocene horse, the modifications that took place in his feet are not steps in evolution.

It can with safety be said that the greater part of the changes that have been found in animals and claimed to be steps in evolution, have been only modifications made by nature to suit them to an environment. These animals, like the eocene horse, did not become more complex; therefore their changes cannot in any way be accredited to biological evolution.

I have been treating the orthodox theory of biological evolution rather roughly over the little eocene horse. It might have been worse had I taken other examples, but the eocene horse theory having been so much written about, it is probably better known to the layman than any other. Now let us see whether I am justified in my harsh treatment of the eocene horse and evolution.

Now first I will show a natural law.

The regular and continued physical use of any member or part of a living body will enlarge, develop and strengthen that member or part.

The regular and continued neglect physically to use and exercise any member or part of a living body results in that member or part becoming weak and shrunken. These are accepted facts by science.

When the eocene horse first came into existence, the ground on which he lived was soft and spongy, and he was supplied with feet to suit the character of the ground. He had five long toes like those of a wading-bird, which prevented his feet from sinking into the soft soil.

The first notable change to be seen in the horse's foot was when the ground was hardening. Then we find the side toes weakening and shrinking, while the center toe especially was enlarging. This at once shows a change in the character of the ground. It was hardening, and nature was adapting the foot of the animal for the changing condition. As the ground hardened, so the toes failed to sink into the soil as heretofore. The center toe, being the longest, was the last to leave the ground when the animal was taking a step, and, for a period in the step, the center toes, sustained the whole weight of the animal. Thus for a space of time the center toe was doing the work of what had hitherto been done by five toes. This extra work on the central toe enlarged and strengthened it, while the work having been taken off the side toes caused them to weaken and to shrink; they became mere digits above and at the back of the central toe. When all of the work fell on the central toe, it strengthened and developed enormously, the nail grew and enlarged to what we now call a hoof. Thus the central toe on each foot with the horn-like hoofs is the only one used by the horse today in its locomotion.

This is the physical side of the so-called "evolution of the horse," which, as I have shown, is mere modification made by nature to suit conditions, and which, in no way, affects the chemical side by altering the elementary compounds. It made the animal neither more nor less complex. The advocate of evolution has yet to bring forward the first particle of proof to uphold his theory of evolution.

Our modern scientists have utterly failed to show the connection between the forces and the elements. Especially prominent is this where life is concerned. Fifty thousand years ago, among the scientists of the earth's first great civilization, this was their most prominent study.

Fortunately for mankind many of our greatest and deepest thinkers have not been robbed of their reason or overwhelmed by the tidal wave of biological evolution.

Alfred Russell Wallace, the great English scientist, and at one time a strong advocate of the evolution theory, in his last work, "World of Life," page 421, says:

"In the present work I have endeavored to suggest a reason which appeals to me as both a sufficient and intelligible one: it is that this earth with its infinite life and beauty and mystery, and the universe in which we are placed, with its overwhelming immensities of suns and nebula, of light and motion, are as they are, firstly, for the development of life culminating in man; secondly, as a vast schoolhouse for the higher education of the human race in preparation for the enduring spiritual life to which it is destined."

Very few human beings believe that man has no soul or no hereafter. Even the poor savages do not believe this. The evolutionist starts when he is confronted with the fact that he believes himself to be only a brute animal. To be a true evolutionist, a man must be an atheist. If a man believes in God, and if he believes he has a soul and a hereafter, he is not an atheist, nor is he an evolutionist. He only thinks he is. He is only professing to believe in evolution to be considered orthodox.

If biological evolution were a fact, there would be no such things as forces, and, a form of life once coming into existence should continue on indefinitely. It should never die out. The great reptilian life would still occupy parts of the earth. If there was no vital or life force, these great tragedies would still be with us, but they are not. Why?

Because there is a life or vital force, and
Because biological evolution is a myth.

Chapter VII. The Sun

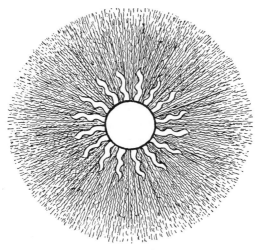

Sun. From a very ancient Hindu writing

THE SUN'S SIZE. Scientists who have made a study of the sun tell us that the diameter of the sun is 832,000 miles, and her circumference is 2,773,000 miles.

How can the actual size of the sun be stated when it is taken into consideration that the actual body of the sun has never been seen? All that can be seen of the sun is the double layer of opaque, impenetrable specialized clouds. The actual thickness of these clouds is unknown. They cannot be measured, their thickness can only be guessed at. Then, beyond these clouds, there is a space between them and the sun filled with dark impenetrable parent rays. The thickness or diameter of this space is unmeasurable. Beyond these parent rays comes the sun. On what basis, with the foregoing facts before me, the sun's size can be measured, I cannot conceive.

It has been advanced by some scientists that sun spots are visions of the actual body of the sun. I do not think so. My belief is that a sun spot is a rift in the clouds, disclosing the dark parent rays coming from the sun before they arrive at the double layer of clouds to be divided and filtered out.

During the passage of the parent rays through the sun's double layer of specialized clouds and the specialized atmosphere, the parent rays are first divided and then filtered out into the separate rays, and then shot through space. Some of these filtered-out rays are of the light variety, others are of the dark ultra-invisible kind of which there are over 90 per cent. This percentage is higher than given in our scientific works, but then, there is a division of these dark rays, so ultra as to become extremes to any possible measurement. I speak of that section of the sun's rays which carry the affinitive forces, affinitive to the forces of her controlling sun, but not affinitive to the forces emanating from the various bodies forming the solar system.

Hershel, the great scientist, who probably made a deeper and more exhaustive study of the sun than any other man, wrote: "Sun spots are the actual body of the sun showing through a rift in the double layer of clouds which surround its body."

I shall now draw a comparison between the sun and the planet Saturn. Saturn has a ring surrounding her body. If this ring was extended in such a manner as to cover her whole body like the specialized clouds cover the sun's body, then Saturn would appear to be many times larger than her actual size.

How much greater is the diameter of the sun's double layer of clouds than her actual body? Has this ever been determined and by what means?

I am impressed with the facts that as the actual body of the sun has never been seen, the thickness of the double layer of opaque clouds surrounding her has never been determined, and the distance between these clouds and the sun's body is unknown, that all conclusions that have been arrived at regarding the size of the sun are subject to correction.

THE SUN'S WEIGHT. Scientists have computed and published the weight of the sun, saying, "The weight of the sun is 730 times the weight of the earth and all the planets combined." How any scientist can associate weight with any celestial body, I cannot comprehend, because in space a body has no weight. In space the largest celestial body has not the weight of a thistledown.

Weight, as it is known, is the measurement of the draw or pull of a cold magnetic force on elements. The force emanates from the body itself. This cold magnetic force attracts and draws the elements of the body toward the magnet from which the force emanates. The power of this attraction represents weight.

As an example we will take the earth. Eliminate the cold magnetic force, and then, regardless of the size or density of the matter, it would have no weight. Walking off the roof of a house, you would float in the air and be incapable of coming to the ground; all loose matter which might leave the surface of the earth would float off and become lost in space until it came into the atmosphere of a revolving body having a cold magnetic force. Then it would be drawn to its surface. Meteorites are an example of this phenomenon.

It is possible that the cold magnetic force of the sun is 730 times stronger than those of the earth and planets combined, but weight? No!

THE SUN'S TEMPERATURE. Scientific works that are orthodox tell us that the sun is "an exceedingly hot, super-heated body."

Herschel did not agree with the orthodox. He wrote: "The sun may be a cool body."

From the various works written about the sun which I have studied, the impression is left that scientists have based their opinions that the sun's body has a very high temperature from readings of the spectrum and on the erroneous belief that:

"The sun disperses her heat throughout the solar system."

and

"The earth's heat comes directly from the sun."

They have made no study to determine what heat is, nor its manner of working. Their writings must therefore be what they are, mere guesses, and very erroneous at that. I have heretofore devoted a section to heat, showing what it is, whence it emanates, and how it works. We meet phenomena at every step showing most conclusively that our heat does not come from the sun but is an earthly force.

Another phenomenon which confirms the fact that we do not derive our heat directly from the sun, and that the sun does not distribute its heat throughout the solar system, as is being taught today in our educational establishments, is shown during the earth's elliptical orbit.

I will take the northern hemisphere as an example. Twice during the year the sun is millions of miles nearer the earth than at other times. During the fall and spring the sun is millions of miles nearer the earth than in the summer. If the sun is the source of heat, when the earth is millions of miles nearer the source we ought to experience a higher temperature during the spring and fall, but do we? We do not! We experience a middle temperature, clearly proving that our heat does not come directly from the sun, thus bearing out the writings that have been handed down to us from the first great civilization.

The deduction that the sun is an exceedingly hot super-heated body has been determined by the spectroscope. This in itself is the greatest absurdity because the spectroscope does not register temperatures. It cannot, because it does not register the rays which carry the heat force. This I personally have proved in a court of law as an expert witness. Our scientists in their writings about the sun have totally ignored the natural workings of the forces. Nature's tools and means have been cast to the winds.

I have made many interesting experiments with the optical pyrometer, which is a form of spectroscope, the foundation of both being a prism. Some of these were given in the section on heat—pages 91–98.

I could go on almost indefinitely with similar demonstrations. The chemical tag $C_{10}H_{16}$ is not in it with the prism. I must reiterate to impress my readers thoroughly that:

It is absolutely impossible to measure temperature with a prism of any form, for this reason: the prism does not record heat-carrying rays. On the other hand, it repels them, because the prism is clear white, the heat-carrying rays are dark; white repels dark as was shown in Tyndall's experiment, pp. 109–110.

The prism records light rays only which carry no heat. Basing mine on Tyndall's, I made the following experiment: First I took a cell filled with a clear solution of alum water, which allowed the free transmission of the light rays with their forces. After passing through the solution with the aid of a lens, I focussed them; then with an optical pyrometer I measured the temperature of the bright spot at the focus point. The pyrometer said it was 2500° F. to 2600° F. I then put an ordinary thermometer at the focus point, letting the focus fall on the bulb of the thermometer. The temperature remained stationary at atmospheric, which was 68° F.

I then changed the cell, using the iodine solution, which allowed the dark rays with their forces free transmission. There was no bright spot at the focus point, and the pyrometer registered no rise over atmospheric. I then placed the bulb of the thermometer at the focus point. The mercury climbed rapidly to the top, then the thermometer burst. And the prism or optical pyrometer is what our scientists have been measuring the temperature of our and other suns with.

The halo of clouds which surround the sun are said to contain elements with which we are acquainted, but with us they are in a solid state. This phenomenon appears to be another reason for our scientists to say the sun is a hot super-heated body. This phenomenon is no criterion whatever. Many of our solid elements can be turned into gaseous clouds without involving high temperatures. Release the oxygen from the oxide and it becomes very simple. Many examples will be found in books on chemistry. Have we not many of the so-called solid elements permeating our atmosphere?

Now comes the question, do these elements actually exist in the sun's clouds and atmosphere? Or are the sun's clouds and atmosphere free of these elements? This is a very open question. I will start by assuming that the spectroscope does actually register these elements. If so, it is by colors naturally. Between the sun's clouds and atmosphere and the spectroscope, the earth's atmosphere intervenes—it comes between the two. All these elements claimed to be in the sun's clouds and atmosphere, analysis tells us exist in the earth's atmosphere. May it not be that the spectroscope is registering that which is in the earth's atmosphere and not anything in the sun's?

A ray partakes of the color of any substance which it passes through. The proofs are: take an incandescent lamp, and let it fall on a sheet of white paper. No color appears. But place colored glasses between the lamp and the paper, red, blue, yellow, green, orange, mauve, or any other color. Directly the colored glass intervenes between the lamp and the paper, the paper changes to the color of the glass, whatever it may be. Apply a similar test with the spectroscope of the sun's clouds and atmosphere, using the earth's atmosphere to represent the colored glass. What will be the result?

THE SUN'S FLAMES. Various scientific works state that:

"The sun is constantly sending forth flames hundreds of
    thousands of miles long."

and

"The heat of the solar system is derived directly from the
    sun."

These two assertions are absolutely untenable. Records show that the ancients of the motherland and the Hindus 25,000 years ago knew better, and their knowledge was confirmed by the Mayas, Nahuatls, and Egyptians of later date.

The sun's so-called flames are rays—rays without heat. They are without heat because they are of the light visible kind which carry no heat.

As the sun's rays which we see are of the light variety and as light rays do not carry heat, it is proof positive that the sun's flashings which we see are cold and therefore not flames.

The sun's body lies within an envelope of specialized clouds, impenetrable by human vision or by present man's devices.

Rays leave the sun's body in the form of dark ultra-invisible

[173]

parent rays. These rays are the carriers of the sun's forces, which forces have been drawn from its body by the affinitive magnetic forces of its superior or governing sun. On passing through the sun's double layer of clouds and atmosphere, these parent rays are divided and filtered out into single rays. Then in the sun's atmosphere, the light division becomes visible to the human eye. Beyond the sun's atmosphere, they cannot be seen, because rays have to pass through an atmosphere to become visible. Atmosphere is composed of elements. Beyond the sun's atmosphere there are no elements, until the atmosphere of the next celestial body is met.

As soon as the sun's rays with their forces arrive at the earth's atmosphere, those forces affinitive to earthly forces commence their work. Thus the sun's rays which are affinitive to the earth's light force set it in motion, and the phenomenon of "daylight" or "sunlight" is the result.

Flames result from the combustion of elements. Flames of the magnitude of the sun's flashings would have consumed the body of the sun many millions of years ago, notwithstanding it may be 832,000 miles in diameter. Then today there would be no sun, and all of the members of the solar system, including the earth, would be dead—aimless wanderers in space.

Flames are super-heated elementary gases coming from a combustion. Combustion is a thermo-analysis of a substance whereby the solid is transformed into elementary gases. Thus, if the scientists are correct, the sun has been deliberately trying to commit suicide for the past millions upon millions of years. The sun is not so foolish as to attempt such a thing. Such a contention therefore cannot be maintained for a moment on either a scientific or any reasonable basis. Therefore:

The sun does not emit huge flames of fire. I have often

wondered whether the scientist who invented "the sun's flames" and those who believe in the invention ever stopped to consider that they are advocating the possibility of elements traveling thousands of times faster than lightning. For, if it is flames that the sun is sending forth, then it must be elements. Some very interesting question could be put to the inventor of the "sun's flames" regarding velocity and resistance, when he asserts that elements can be made to travel faster than forces. That is, elements can be made to travel thousands of times faster than lightning. Earthly examples of the sun's flashings are the Borealis and an ordinary searchlight. Both are cold. There is no heat in either of them. Combustion is unnecessary to produce visible rays, for visible rays emanate from our radio-active elements when they are cold, such as radium, uranium, and thorium, also from fireflies, glowworms, and some fishes.

It is impossible that the bodies of the solar system can obtain their heat from the sun, because heat is a force that requires room space in elements, and without elements heat cannot exist; between the sun and the various bodies of the solar system, there are tens of millions of miles of space without elementary matter, simply an essence. Over these gulfs there are no bridges. How is heat going to get across?

All creations are duplications. It would therefore appear to be a fact beyond controversy that the great rays and their forces are drawn from the sun by the governing sun, and in a manner similar to that in which the electro-magnetic division of the earth's primary force are drawn from her body by the affinitive forces of the sun. Of the fact that the sun's forces are being drawn from its body by the affinitive magnetic forces of its governing sun there is proof positive in the fact that the sun's poles oscillate and the sun revolves on her axis.

The sun's polar regions must be regularly magnetized and de-magnetized, otherwise the poles could not oscillate. This phenomenon is explained in section, "The Earth's Pendulum," page 196.

Earthly forces are constantly being drawn from the earth's body out into the atmosphere by affinitive forces of the sun. We can neither see these forces leave the earth's body, nor can we see them when out in the atmosphere. The effects of the sun's forces are seen in her atmosphere. This may be due to either the specialized character of her atmosphere or to her volume or both. Although volumes of forces constantly leave the earth's body, we do not see their effect because the volume is too low to cause incandescence in the atmosphere. It is only when the atmosphere becomes overcharged and the surplus aggregates, concentrates, and returns to the earth, that we see any effect.

There is the possibility that the sun's flashings which we see may be the incandescence of her atmosphere caused by a sufficient volume of forces passing through it at a sufficient velocity to cause its incandescence.

THE SUN'S ATMOSPHERE. It is quite reasonable to assume that the sun has a very much specialized atmosphere, in many respects similar to the earth's atmosphere, only much more highly specialized.

Again, without question the sun's atmosphere extends an immense distance from her double layer of clouds. Her atmosphere no doubt extends out far beyond the limit of her flashings, because it requires a certain amount of density to become incandescent.

I do not think anything of a definite nature is known about the sun's atmosphere. There have been many scientific guesses, but when analyzed, they all show that they are guesses and speculations pure and simple. All lack a foundation.

THE SUN'S MOVEMENTS. Drayson, writing, says:

"The sun is revolving around a center and is traveling at the rate of 40 miles per second, 3,456,000 miles per hour, and 1,264,440,000 miles during one of our years."

"The sun's orbit is 33,000,000,000,000,000 miles."

"Our sun takes 71,000 years to make her orbit around her governing sun."

Proctor, writing, says:

"The sun revolves on her axis once in 16 days of our time."

"The sun's poles oscillate once in every 11 years of our time."

The foregoing from noted scientists gives all of the essential points for argument and demonstration that I require.

Proctor states that 11 years of our time constitutes one sun's year. Some scientists may object to my interpretation of Proctor's writings and say that one sun's year constitutes a complete orbit around her governing sun. Against this is a complete oscillation of the sun's poles, thereby giving the four seasons if she has seasons. If Drayson's figures are correct and Proctor's as well, then it takes the sun 6500 of her own years to make her orbit around her governing sun.

The poles of a sphere might oscillate any number of times during a circuit around her governing sun, and each complete oscillation would constitute a year. I have been unable to find any scientist stating the number of degrees the sun's poles travel from their mean position. Virtually all scientists agree on the following:

The sun revolves on her axis.

and

The sun's poles oscillate.

In these two facts is a foundation to work upon to show and

[177]

determine beyond all doubt and controversy the actual temperature of the sun.

First we must see what conditions are necessary to enable a sphere to revolve on its axis where magnetic forces are the agents involved.

A spherical body to revolve on its axis through the agency of forces must be governed by a superior body.

The superior body must also be revolving on its axis to generate controlling forces. To enable a sphere to revolve on her axis, it must be generating affinitive magnetic forces.

Some, at least, of the magnetic forces emanating from each of the bodies must be affinitive to each other.

For a sphere to generate magnetic forces by revolving, the sphere must have a hard outside crust and a soft center. Otherwise no frictional line could be established, and without a frictional line, no forces could be generated or regenerated.

The sun revolves on her axis,

therefore

The sun has a hard crust and a soft center.

As the crust of the sun is hard, it is impossible that she can be the hot super-heated body claimed by scientists, because, if she were, her elementary body would be quickly turned into gases, and she would become a nebula, without a frictional line and generating no forces of any description. A nebula has no poles, therefore she could not spin on her axis. Revolving gases do not produce governing forces. Herschel was right when he wrote "The sun may be a cool body." It is. His only error was he did not bring forth reasonable proofs to uphold his theory. His was an omission and not a scientific sin.

Forces cannot exist in a super-heated body. They require a cool storehouse. Neither can they be generated or regenerated in anything but a super-heated frictional line.

I think the foregoing is supplying reasonable proofs that The sun is a cool body.

Therefore she is not an exceedingly hot super-heated body. Being a cool body, she does not disperse heat throughout the solar system. Furthermore

All revolving bodies throughout the universe are cool bodies.

By cool I do not mean frigid. I mean that their surface temperatures are not sufficiently high to melt elements, turning them into gases, but low enough for generated forces to be stored in.

If further proof is wanted that the sun is a cool body, it will be found in Chapter VII on pages 170–171. There I have shown that heat is an earthly force. This is not a new discovery. It is only a re-discovery, being well known to our forefathers, the scientists of the earth's first great civilization, tens of thousands of years ago.

Our sun's governing sun has never been seen, and probably never will be for the following reasons: First, according to Drayson it would be 12,000,000,000,000,000 miles away, which is beyond the reach of our telescopes. If Drayson is right, then all of the celestial bodies which we see are under this superior sun's control.

Second, to control such a system, forces would be generated so intense as to be beyond all of our imagination, and such forces could only be carried in the intense invisible dark rays. Thus a black halo would surround her body, making her body invisible. She being invisible, her rays would pass through space unseen and unknown except for their effect on the celestial bodies which we can see.

THE SUN'S FORCES. As the sun has a hard crust and a soft

or molten center, and is revolving on its axis, it no doubt is generating forces somewhat similar to those generated by the earth. On account of the sun's size and velocity, the forces generated by her must necessarily be far more intense and powerful than the forces generated by the earth.

Magnetic forces are being generated, since the sun has a central frictional line.

Light forces are being generated, because they show in her atmosphere; also she has light forces, which are affinitive to the earth's light force.

Heat forces are being generated, because she has heat forces which are affinitive to the earth's heat force.

A centrifugal force is being generated, because she is a revolving sphere.

A gyroscopical force is being generated, as shown by the oscillation of her poles.

Her crust is hard and cool, because she stores magnetic forces in it for her superior sun to draw on and revolve her, and because her polar regions are being super-magnetized and de-magnetized, as shown by the oscillation of her poles.

As our sun revolves on her axis, she has a governing sun, whose forces are infinitely stronger than the forces of our sun.

The forces of the governing sun must be affinitive to some of the forces of our sun, but not to all, because if the forces of the governing sun were affinitive to all of our sun's forces, then the governing sun's forces would be affinitive to earthly forces. Then, the forces of the governing sun being so much more powerful than those of our sun, the governing sun's forces would draw the earth and all the planets out of the solar system and bring them under her own direct control. We should then revolve around the governing sun instead of our own. As we are not under the direct control of the governing sun, it shows that the earth's forces are neutral to those of the governing sun. It also shows that our sun is generating intense forces which are neutral to the earth's, but affinitive to those of the governing sun. It is the dark, ultra-invisible rays which carry these intense forces of the sun, which I have referred to when I said the dark radiation from our sun was over 90 per cent of her total radiation.

A celestial body which does not revolve on her axis cannot possibly be generating any forces. She is a dead one. The body will have forces, but, like her elements, they will be latent and inactive. All elements are associated with forces, and all forces are associated with elements. Even a non-revolving body has forces, but they are inactive, bottled up, so to speak.

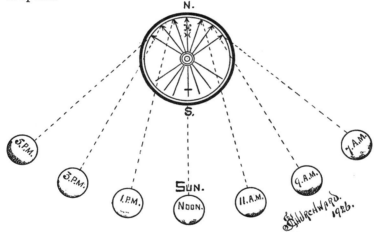

The sun's forces drawing a magnetic needle

"THE SUN IS A MAGNET." Proctor, writing, says: "The sun is a magnet."

Of course the sun is a magnet. How could it be otherwise? For all of the forces which the sun is sending through the solar system are magnetic, with one exception—her centrifugal force.

Proctor quotes the variations of the magnetic needle during the hours of sunlight by saying:

"The magnetic needle makes an effort during the hours of sunlight to turn towards the sun. When the sun is at its meridian, the magnetic needle has its mean position."

"There is an extreme and a minimum variation of the magnetic needle during a period of 11 years."

During the morning hours, the needle is drawn towards the east. At noon it points due north, and in the afternoon it dips towards the west, as shown in my cut. In this cut the movements of the needle are very much exaggerated, so the picture must be looked upon as typical rather than actual. It is thus drawn so that the movements of the needle may be thoroughly understood.

On page 181 I showed what the magnetic needle was and that it contained a super-volume of a magnetic force coming out of the electro-magnetic division of the primary force. All forces in this division are extremely affinitive to certain of the sun's forces—so that the force in the magnetic needle was attracted and drawn by all of the sun's affinitive forces. While the effect of the sun's forces on the needle shows affinity, it does not show the actual reason why the needle moves towards the sun.

All affinitive forces and all single forces, when scattered, endeavor on all occasions to join and aggregate. This is especially noticeable in a single scattered force, and is demonstrated when two bodies, each containing a volume of the same force, apparently unaided by anything tangible, draw together and attach themselves to one another. With the magnetic needle, the force in it is attempting to leave the needle to join and aggregate with the sun's affinitive force. This it is unable to do because the elements composing the needle have a greater power over it than the sun's affinitive force. The needle being balanced on the fine point of a thin pillar reduces the friction caused by its swing to the minimum. Although the sun's force cannot overcome the resistance of the elements, it can and does overcome the friction.

Like the magnetic needle, an ordinary magnet has a supervolume of the same magnetic force as the needle. If, as I said, a scattered force always attempts to join and aggregate, the magnet should be enabled to affect the needle. Let us see by making the magnet a little sun. As the magnet is brought towards the needle, the needle swings and points towards the magnet. The force in the needle is endeavoring to join the force in the magnet. If the magnet is swung to and fro, the needle follows the movement of the magnet. Take the magnet completely around the box and the needle will follow it, making a complete circle. The magnet is controlling the movements of the needle, but is incapable of drawing the force out of it.

Proctor mentions:

"The discovery that the periodical changes of the sun's appearance are associated with the periodic change in the character of the earth's magnetism. . . ."

Proctor here has undoubtedly inadvertently used a wrong word by saying "character" of magnetism. What he undoubtedly meant was degree.

Magnetism is a force. There are various magnetic forces. The character of a force never changes, but various magnetic forces have various characteristics; some are affinitive to other forces only, while others are also affinitive to elements; so that if "character" stands, it would mean one class of magnetic forces would supplant and take the place of others. In my mind Proctor certainly meant degree and used "character" in error, which would be quite easy to do if one allows the theme to be in any way broken in a line of thought. The phenomenon which Proctor speaks of is that the earth's magnetism varies in degree.

Proctor:

"The deviation of the magnetic needle is greatest during the period of 11 years at the time when sun spots are most numerous and of the greatest area."

Here we have an exceedingly interesting phenomenon upon which many a theory could be advanced. First, it would be necessary to know the positions of the sun's poles when "sun spots are most numerous and of the greatest area." As the sun oscillates her poles once in 11 years, and the sun spots occur during one particular period in these 11 years, it is self-evident that they either occur when the sun's pole is dipped towards the earth, when it is pointing away from the earth, or when it is in its mean position.

Basing a theory that "sun spots are most numerous and of the greatest area" when the sun's pole is dipped towards the earth, many phenomena are apparently accounted for.

The sun's polar regions like the earth's are super-magnetized; when the pole is dipped towards the earth, it would bring a greater surface of the sun's super-magnetized area exposed to the earth. Consequently a greater volume of super-magnetized rays and forces. This is one possibility.

The sun's double layer of clouds may be more dense around her equatorial regions than in her polar regions. In other words, they may taper in density from the equatorial regions to the poles. Then when the pole is at its extreme dip towards the earth, rifts or openings may appear in the thinner and less dense polar clouds. These rifts or openings would appear black and be what is called sun spots. These openings would not expose the body of the sun, as suggested by Herschel, but the dark invisible parent rays which surround and envelop her body, making the body unseen to the human eye. Through such rifts or openings, we should therefore receive direct the parent rays of the sun unfiltered or undiluted. These rays would be more intense than what we ordinarily receive, consequently would have greater power to affect the magnetic needle. Then, once in every 11 years, the magnetic needle would be subject to a greater deviation.

An interesting experiment to make, if it were possible, would be to test the rays coming from sun spots, without involving the other rays coming from the sun, and see whether rays coming from sun spots only are capable of affecting the earth's light force. If the rays from sun spots are incapable of doing so, then we know at once that the sun's specialized clouds and atmosphere are necessary to the production of light on earth.

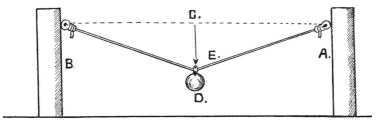

Action of sun's forces on magnetic needle

By a diagram I will now show how and why the magnetic needle is deflected by the sun's magnetic affinitive forces.

To obtain the force represented by A as being anchored in the compass, the weight D must break it away from its fastening. This it cannot do. It does, however, pull the line down and deflects it from a straight line to B. The deflection in the cord represents the deflection of the magnetic needle.

The variation of the magnetic needle caused by the sun's affinitive magnetic force is a convincing natural phenomenon that:

The sun has powerful magnetic forces,

The earth has powerful magnetic forces; and

That some of the sun's magnetic forces are affinitive to some of the earth's magnetic forces.

THE SOLAR SYSTEM. I have taken the solar system as an example of how all systems throughout the universe probably work. In fact they must either work in the same manner or very like it to avoid collisions among the celestial bodies.

The distance from the earth to the sun has been calculated to be about 91,430,000 miles. The length of her annual circuit around the sun is stated to be about 609,553,000 miles. The earth is traveling in this circuit at a rate of about 1,670,000 miles per day. The earth makes her orbit around the sun in the form of an ellipse. There is no visible connection between the earth and the sun whereby the earth is being held in given distances from the sun. This being the case, it demonstrates that unseen forces are the agents and that these forces emanate from the sun.

To accomplish this orbit by the agency of forces, more than one force is required. It is also shown that all forces are working in harmony and unison. I shall now attempt to show what the forces are, how they are generated, and how they work,—a stupendous attempt, but after over 50 years' study of the subject, I think I can accomplish it.

For the sun to carry the earth around herself in an orbit, four separate and distinct forces are required.

Three of these must emanate from the sun, and

One from the earth.

The four forces are:

A sun's propellent force to carry the earth along in her orbit.

A sun's repellent force to prevent the earth from being drawn into the sun.

A sun's magnetic force to prevent the repellent force from carrying the earth out into space.

An earthly magnetic force or forces that are affinitive to the sun's propellent and magnetic forces.

It may involve two earthly magnetic forces or only one, I cannot say.

I have heretofore shown that all these forces exist. Two of the sun's forces, the magnetic and repellent, must form a neutral zone. The repellent force at the sun's surface must be stronger than the magnetic force, and from the sun's surface must diminish in strength as it works out into space. The magnetic must be weaker at the sun's surface than the repellent and also diminish in strength as it moves out into space, but the rate at which its power diminishes must be much slower than that of the repellent; then, at a given point, dependent on the magnetic capacity of the planet, a neutral zone will be formed, from which she cannot stray.

Each of the planets has a different magnetic capacity. Therefore, as their magnetism differs, so must their neutral zones differ in distance from the sun. Thus it is shown why Mercury is so close to the sun and Neptune so far away as to be out of sight.

Apparently, I cannot say it authoritatively, the magnetic capacity is governed by density. If our scientists are correct in their assertions about the densities of the planets, the planet nearest to the sun is the densest and the farthest one away the least dense of all.

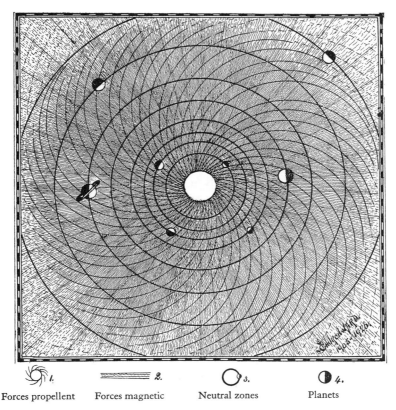

Forces propellent   Forces magnetic   Neutral zones   Planets

THE SOLAR SYSTEM

This is a conventional diagram. Distances and sizes are not considered.

1. Curved lines radiating from the sun. The centrifugal force.
2. Straight and wavey lines. The sun's forces, including magnetic.
3. Black circles. The neutral zones of the planets.
4. The planets. _____

I shall now show how the various forces must work.

THE PROPELLENT. The propellent force is achieved by the attraction and holding power, one to the other, of certain of the sun's magnetic forces and certain of the earth's magnetic forces belonging to the electro-magnetic division. The sun's rays with their forces follow the spinning movement of the sun, like spokes in a wheel when it revolves, following the hub. The sun is the hub, and the rays with their forces are the spokes. It is also illustrated by changing the angle of a searchlight; the rays from the searchlight follow the change of angle.

The forces in the sun's rays attach themselves to the earth's affinitive forces in a manner to the various illustrations already given. The strength of this magnetic bond is sufficient to hold the earth in touch and carry her around in her orbit. Neither the earth or any of the planets travel forward as fast as the sun's rays. If they did, they would make their orbits in 16 days.

The magnetic grip, however, is not sufficient to hold either the earth or any of the planets rigid. There is what is termed in mechanical machinery a slippage. This so-called slippage is due to two facts: actual slippage and the actual breakage of connections. As the earth or a planet revolves, as the area passes on from sight of the sun, the actual contact is broken, as one surface disappears from the sun another surface comes forward in view, so that as one connection is broken another one is made.

A magnetic slippage can be demonstrated by passing a magnet around the box of a magnetic needle swiftly. The needle will follow the magnet but lose ground all the time, and eventually go out of control entirely unless another magnet follows the first. Then the forward movement of the needle will be continued, corresponding to new areas being

[189]

brought forward, to be brought under the magnetic hold.

A phenomenon in connection with the magnetic needle is that the further away from the needle the magnet is, the slower will be the movements of the needle. So it is with the planets and the sun, the farther away from the sun the planet is, the slower her movements are found to be.

The momentum of the earth must also be taken into consideration, although almost infinitesimal, as she has no weight in space.

The moon and the planet Mercury are examples of pure magnetic slippage. As neither revolves on her axis and as neither travels at the rate of the forces controlling their orbits, pure slippage accounts for their tardiness. The sun's principal magnetic hold on the earth is the area of the polar regions, which are super-magnetized. The sun has no hold whatever on a de-magnetized region.

THE REPELLENT. The repellent force is the sun's centrifugal force, which is always casting off, throwing outwards and away from the place of generation; it endeavors to throw everything within its reach out into space, and to throw all of the sun's satellites off beyond her reach and control. This, however, it cannot do because there is another force working against it. This force tries to draw every satellite into the sun; to avoid either catastrophe, the Great Designer instituted neutral zones, where the forces are equal in power, so that the repellent force cannot throw the earth and planets out into space.

THE MAGNETIC. The magnetic force is one of the sun's magnetic forces. I say one because the sun has ultra and intense magnetic forces, which are affinitive to the forces of her governing sun, and which are not affinitive to earthly forces. This I have previously shown.

Whether it is the sun's magnetic force which is carrying the earth in her orbit, the magnetic force which turns the earth on her axis, or a totally different one that is antagonistic to the repellent force, I am not prepared to say.

The sun's magnetic forces undoubtedly reach beyond the outermost satellite, whatever that may be. Neptune may or may not be the last out. The recently discovered Pluto may or may not be a member of our solar system.

From the movements shown by the bodies comprising the solar system, it is self-evident that the repellent force is much stronger at the sun's surface than the magnetic force, and that as they both work out into space the repellent loses its power much faster than the magnetic.

NEUTRAL ZONES. The neutral zones of the earth and planets are shown in the diagram of the solar system, page 188 as circles parallel to the sun with a planet on each circle. The neutral zone of a satellite is governed by her magnetic capacity. Her magnetic capacity in turn is governed by the elements composing the body, the thickness of the crust, and the general density. This is fully verified by the bodies composing the solar system.

The higher or greater the magnetic capacity of a planet is, the nearer will be her neutral zone to the sun, and the body with the lowest magnetic capacity will have its neutral zone the farthest away from the sun.

A body, when given an impetus by a temporary force, flies forward, commencing in a straight line, and continues on in this straight line until some magnetic force attracts it, and eventually stops it having overcome a temporary force. Then the magnetic force claims the body.

If, however, the propellent force is not of a temporary character, and of a circular movement, with sufficiently strong centrifugal and magnetic forces governing it, so as to form a neutral zone, then the flight must be everlasting.

As this is the condition in which the earth and planets are placed, their flights around the sun must continue on to the end of time.

As an example showing the difference between a temporary and an everlasting force, I will take a grindstone with its underside in a trough of water.

As the grindstone revolves, the water in the trough is picked up by it, carried a little distance, and then thrown off by the grindstone's centrifugal temporary force. The water, as it leaves the wheel, starts off in a straight line, but soon commences to curve towards the earth. This curve is an indication that the earth's everlasting cold magnetic force is claiming the water and is overcoming the grindstone's centrifugal force. At last the water strikes the earth. A weakened temporary force has succumbed to a strong everlasting force.

Neither the earth or any of the planets can be carried out into space any more than the water could be carried out into space by the grindstone's centrifugal force.

The earth and planets can be carried out by the sun's centrifugal force just so far and no further. They are compelled each and all to remain in their neutral zones. For at the distance from the sun at which they are placed, the sun's magnetic force is holding them against the sun's centrifugal force. Neither the earth or any of the planets can be drawn into the sun, for, within their neutral zones, the sun's repellent force is stronger than the magnetic, and prevents their nearer approach to the sun.

The earth and each of the planets have their own separate degrees of magnetic capacity, and all being different, no two have the same neutral zone. Therefore they cannot collide with each other.

To have two planets occupying the same neutral zone, it would be necessary to have the two bodies of identically the same size, composed of identically the same element, and in the same exact proportion one to the other, and with identically the same thickness of crust. Otherwise, their magnetic capacity would not be the same; not being the same, it is impossible for them to have the same neutral zone.

I have often been asked, "What would be the result if a planet through some unaccountable cause strayed out of her neutral zone?" Nothing serious could happen. I shall give a diagram showing how the forces would work in such a case and what would eventually become of her. See page 194.

A STRAYING PLANET. I have given two full erroneous circuits and a part of a third before the planet finally settles back again to her neutral zone. As a matter of fact, she might correct her error on the first circuit or it might take many. The whole thing is merely a problem of what would happen if such an error did actually occur.

At the outer circle C the magnetic force would be so much more powerful than the repellent, that the outward progress of the planet would be checked, and she would be brought back with great impetus. This would result in her being brought within the neutral zone at about the center of her orbit. Here the repellent force would gain the ascendency, resulting in sending her out again beyond the neutral zone, but not so far as in her first error, and so it would go on, each time reducing the ellipse until finally she settled down again in her neutral zone.

As an example, take a swinging pendulum; the impetus given at the start keeps the pendulum swinging, but each swing becomes shorter and shorter, until it finally stops. It is then in a neutral zone between the bar on which it swings and the cold magnetic force.

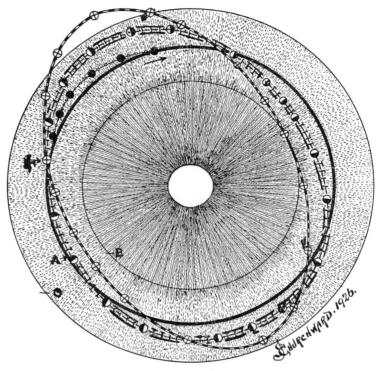

A straying planet

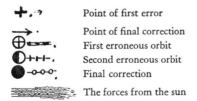

✚, ⇀	Point of first error
⟶ ·	Point of final correction
⊕━━,	First erroneous orbit
◑+++-,	Second erroneous orbit
●-o-o-,	Final correction
≋≋≋	The forces from the sun

The movements of the various bodies throughout the universe clearly show that the solar system is a duplication of the

[194]

many other systems throughout the universe. Our sun with her satellites is moving around a superior sun. This superior sun, with her various systems, is moving around some greater sun, and so on to the center of the universe.

DEDUCTIONS. All forces connected with the earth's circuit around the sun are even and everlasting.

The earth cannot stop her flight around the sun as long as the sun continues to be a living body.

The earth cannot be drawn into the sun.

The earth cannot be hurled off into space.

The earth cannot collide with any other body.

Each body in the solar system has its neutral zone.

Each body in the universe has its neutral zone.

No two neutral zones cross each other.

No body can be drawn out of its neutral zone.

The sun has a hard crust and a soft center.

The sun is not committing slow suicide by burning up.

The sun is a cool body.

The sun supplies no heat beyond her atmosphere.

A pole may be magnetized and de-magnetized many times during a circuit around the governing body.

I have very inadequately shown what the great Cosmic Forces are and their manner of working, but trust that at least some who read this work will find it sufficiently explicit to understand what I wish to convey.

Chapter VIII. Sundry Phenomena

I HAVE called the phenomenon of the oscillation of the earth's pole the earth's pendulum, because the oscillation of the pole is an exact duplication of a clock's swinging pendulum.

Today we find the earth's poles swinging in a methodical and regular manner. The poles of the earth complete one oscillation during each revolution around the sun. There is no variation in the oscillation of the poles. They are always exact to a degree and to an hour, proving the earth to be in final magnetic balance.

The journey of the north pole is from about 23½° east of mean to about 23½° west of mean—about 47° in all; forward and back again from 23½° E. to 23½° W. and back again constitutes one complete oscillation.

These forward and backward movements of the pole give us our four seasons of the year.

The diagram given is intended to cover the northern regions of the Northern Hemisphere, extending a little south of the Arctic Circle.

To accomplish the oscillation of the pole, the workings of the forces are as follows:

Starting with the pole at its western limit, 23½° west of mean. For some months the sun's rays have not fallen on the northern polar regions, and for some distance south the sun has only shone on this area but a few hours during each day and then her rays were at the most obtuse angles. During these months all of these regions have become super-magnetized, as virtually during this period no forces have been drawn from the earth's body out into the atmosphere, yet all the time the forces have been thrown into it. Thus it becomes super-magnetized.

When the gyroscopical force last carried the pole back from 23½° east, the pole did not stop at mean—the impetus and

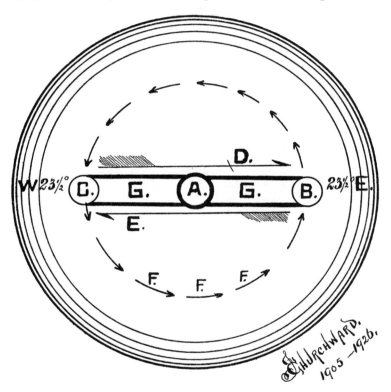

THE EARTH'S PENDULUM

A. The pole's mean position. B. Its easterly limit in travel 23½° east of mean. C. Its westerly limit in travel 23½° west of mean. D. Travelling from west to east. E. Travelling from east to west. F.F.F. The path of a pole of a top—a child's toy. G.G. The path of the earth's pole.

[197]

The clock's pendulum is a duplication of the earth's pendulum

velocity carried it to 23½° west. At 23½° W., the gyroscopical force again got control of the pole and proceeded to carry it back to its mean position, but, as the pole proceeded easterly, it brought the super-magnetized areas in touch with the sun's rays. The sun's forces then began to give an extra strong pull on the polar regions. The power of the gyroscopical force was again overcome, this time by the sun's magnetic affinitive forces. They succeeded in drawing the pole forward to $23\frac{1}{2}°$ east. By the time the pole had arrived at this position, the polar regions had become so far de-magnetized and by it the sun's pull so weakened, that the gyroscopical force again got control of the pole. It then proceeded to carry it back to mean with the same result as before. And so it has been going on and will continue to so go on to the end of time.

The north pole regions are super-magnetized and then de-magnetized, the pole moving during the operation forward and backward like the pendulum of a clock.

If the polar regions did not become super-magnetized so that the sun's forces could get a stronger grip on this part of the earth's surface than on her central areas, the earth would spin without the poles oscillating and there would be no seasonal changes.

If the earth's gyroscopical force was sufficiently strong to overcome the sun's magnetic affinitive forces, then the poles would not oscillate, and there would be no change in temperatures during the year.

If the earth's central magnet was sufficiently strong to hold the earth's forces in her body against the pull of the sun, then the earth would be a dead world. She would not revolve on her axis and no life could exist upon her.

I have been asked why the earth's north pole does not go around in a circle like the pole of a child's top instead of to and fro like the pendulum of a clock.

This is an exceedingly interesting question to answer because the forces operating in both cases are gyroscopical and magnetic.

[199]

First as to the difference. The earth's pole oscillates like the pendulum of a clock as shown in diagram A.B.C., page 198. The top's pole circles as shown by f.f.f. on the diagram.

The force spinning the top is a temporary force. Therefore the top's gyroscopical force is also a temporary one. The gyroscopical force governing the earth's poles is not a temporary one, but an everlasting one.

Both gyroscopical forces, the earth's and the top's, have magnetic forces working against them.

The earth's gyroscopical force has the sun's affinitive magnetic forces pulling against it on one side only, that is, the side facing the sun.

The top's gyroscopical force has the earth's cold magnetic force pulling against it on all sides, for the top is spinning on top of the force and is completely surrounded by it; thus, the top is being pulled down on all sides, while the earth is being pulled on one side only.

The impetus of the spinning top gradually dies down as the temporary force which started it spinning becomes exhausted, and, as the impetus and velocity die down, so the gyroscopical force is weakened in ratio. With the weakening of the top's gyroscopical force, the earth's cold magnetic force begins to claim the top. The cold magnetic starts with pulling the pole over little by little; it gradually succumbs to the magnetic pull. The pole cannot return because the magnetic force is stronger than the gyroscopical, so the magnetic force gains in ratio to the weakening of the gyroscopical force, until finally the gyroscopical force becomes so weak, the magnetic force gets full control and pulls the top over. As the magnetic force pulls the top's pole over, so it holds it, so that the top's pole runs round in circles, the circles becoming larger and larger as the gyroscopical force weakens. The top rolls over and rests on its side, this being the greatest area that can be presented to the central magnet.

The sun's forces are everlasting. The earth's gyroscopical force is everlasting. The earth's gyroscopical force can neither be weakened or stopped. The sun's pull against it is limited and gradually weakens as the pole is arriving at the danger point; the earth's gyroscopical force gets control of it and proceeds to carry it back to mean. The earth, unlike the top, cannot roll over, and as the pull on the earth's gyroscopical force is from one side only, the pole is compelled to follow the pull. Therefore it is forward and backward—see-saw—like the pendulum of a clock.

THE FOUR SEASONS. The earth's temperatures are governed by the angle at which the sun's rays with their forces fall upon her surface. Therefore the oscillation of the earth's poles is responsible for our seasonal changes.

The diagram given illustrates the four seasons. Page 202.

1. The sun is shown vertical on the equator. At this time when the pole is traveling east, it is spring in the northern temperate zones. When the pole is traveling west and the sun is vertical on the equator, it is fall in the northern temperate zone and spring in the southern.

2. The sun is here shown vertical on Cancer. It is now mid-summer in the northern temperate zones and mid-winter in the southern. The angles at which the sun's rays fall on the northern temperate zones are obtuse, while they are most obtuse in the southern.

3. The sun is now vertical on Capricorn, which makes the sun's rays fall on the southern temperate regions at an obtuse angle, and most obtuse in the southern, so that all temperatures have been reversed since the sun left the Tropic of Cancer and moved down to Capricorn, making summer in the

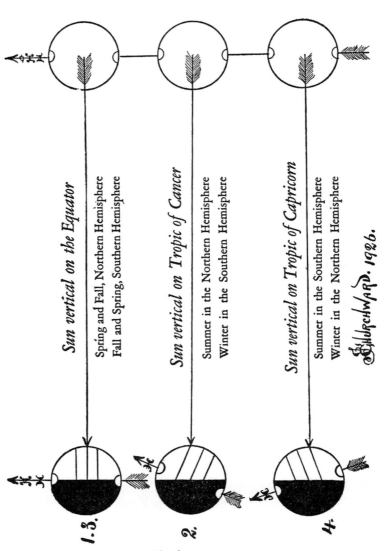

Sun vertical on the Equator

Spring and Fall, Northern Hemisphere
Fall and Spring, Southern Hemisphere

Sun vertical on Tropic of Cancer

Summer in the Northern Hemisphere
Winter in the Southern Hemisphere

Sun vertical on Tropic of Capricorn

Summer in the Southern Hemisphere
Winter in the Northern Hemisphere

CHURCHWARD. 1926.

The four seasons

southern temperate regions and winter in the north.

If the earth revolved at a greater velocity than she is now doing, it would increase the power of the gyroscopical force. This force would then get control before it got to 23½° east of mean. This would shorten the oscillation. If the oscillation were shortened, we should not enjoy the great variations in temperature now experienced in the temperate and frigid zones. These areas would become much colder, and the tropical regions much hotter.

If the earth revolved slower than she is now doing, the power of the earth's gyroscopical force would be reduced. The poles would then have a slower and a longer oscillation, and it would take more than a circuit around the sun for the earth to complete an oscillation, resulting in a longer and a hotter summer, and a longer and a colder winter. It would not end at this only, for it would result in magnetic cataclysms, wiping out the bulk of life, which has been done many times during the earth's development.

All forces connected with the movements of the earth have neutral zones. They are uninfluenced by any forces coming from other suns outside of the solar system. All forces are finally settled, therefore the seasons cannot alter.

They have been as they are now since the time when the earth went into final magnetic balance, and will so remain to the end.

THE EARTH'S ELLIPSE. The earth does not move around the sun in a true circle, but in the form of an ellipse or oval.

Twice during her circuit around the sun, the sun is nearer to it than at other times. When nearest to the sun, the earth is said to be in perihelion.

This occurs during the months of March and September.

Twice during the year the earth is further away from the

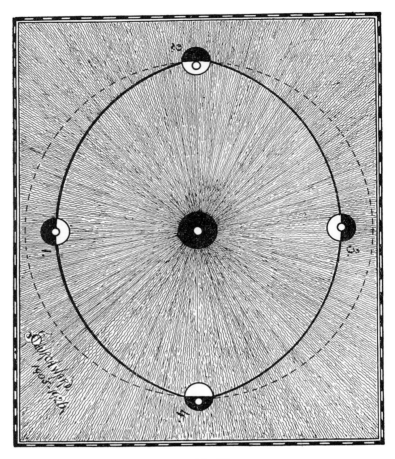

The earth's ellipse

sun than at other times. When farthest away from the sun, the earth is in aphelion. The earth is aphelion in the months of June and December.

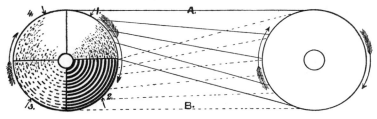

The earth's spin

THE EARTH'S SPIN. The earth's spin or revolution on her axis is accomplished by the working of two sets of forces:

The sun's affinitive magnetic forces, and

The earth's forces affinitive to the sun's magnetic forces and the earth's great central magnet.

Explanation of diagram:

1. One quarter of the earth being de-magnetized by the sun's affinitive magnetic forces (morning).

2. One quarter of the earth de-magnetized so that the sun's forces have no further power over this area from noon to sunset.

3. One quarter of the earth being re-magnetized from sunset till morning.

4. One quarter of the earth completing the re-magnetizing from midnight on to sunrise.

5. Rays carrying effective pulling forces.

6. Rays carrying non-effective pulling forces, as they fall on the de-magnetized quarter; all available forces in this area have been drawn out of the body of the earth into the atmosphere.

To turn the earth on her axis, the affinitive magnetic forces of the sun attract and draw the earth's affinitive forces, which are in the body of the earth. These earthly affinitive forces are the electro-magnetic division of the earth's primary force.

While the sun's forces are pulling on the earthly forces which are in her body, trying to get them out into the atmosphere, the earth's great central magnet tries to prevent it and holds them in the earth's hard crust with all its power and force, thus refusing to let them leave their storehouse without a struggle. Thus there are two forces struggling against each other, a tug-of-war of forces.

The sun's power, however, is greater than the power of the earth's central magnet, and, eventually, after an intense struggle, succeeds in drawing these housed forces from the actual body of the earth out into her atmosphere. The central magnet does not relinquish its claim on the housed forces suddenly but gradually. When the strain by the sun's forces becomes greater than the magnet can resist, they gradually leave the body of the earth.

Some of our scientific brethren may ask the question, "How can we know that the earth's forces are drawn out gradually and not suddenly?" The answer is, "Reason." From the time the sun's forces begin to fall upon the earth's surface, which is at sunrise, they begin to pull on the earth's housed forces, but owing to the obtuse angle at which the sun's forces are pulling, they can only pull on but they cannot draw out the forces from the earth's body. They have, however, sufficient power to pull the earth around until the force in the earth's body is at a sufficiently direct angle, the sun's forces overcome the central magnet and the force is drawn out into the atmosphere. This de-magnetizes this particular surface of the earth, for the magnetic forces have left the earth's body and are out in the atmosphere. When de-magnetized, the sun's forces have no more power over it, because they are not affinitive to elements, and elements only are left. In the meantime, this surface has been pulled forward from the west to the east.

As quarter 1 in the diagram becomes gradually drawn forward and de-magnetized, so quarter 4 is gradually brought forward and takes the place of quarter 1. Thus as one de-magnetized surface passes on, another fully magnetized takes its place. In this way an unbroken, continuous and everlasting pull and revolving goes on.

If there were no resistance to the sun's pull by the central magnet and elementary attraction, the sun would draw the forces out of the earth's body without moving her in any way. If the sun failed to de-magnetize the surface, there would be a neutral zone or dead center, for the sun's forces would have equal power over quarters 1 and 2. This would result in 1 being pulled east and 2 being pulled west; the two surfaces being equal, the two pulls would be equal. Hence the dead center. The earth would then be stationary, that is, having one side only, all the time, towards the sun.

As before stated, when the forces are drawn out of the earth's surface that particular area is de-magnetized and the sun has no more power over it until it becomes re-magnetized.

As soon as an area of the earth has passed on beyond the sun's rays, quarter 3, the sun's forces have disappeared. Then that particular surface commences to re-magnetize. The disappearance of the sun's rays leave the forces in the air or on the surface of the earth to work against the central magnet.

The central magnet then commences to draw back all exhausted forces, and also those nearly exhausted, for re-generation; at the same time it is again filling up the empty storehouse with newly re-generated forces.

Forces which are not exhausted remain in the atmosphere to carry on nature's work during the night. The foregoing does not include the return to earth of atmospheric overcharges like lightning. These forces are not exhausted forces.

I shall now illustrate the foregoing with a couple of examples:

Example 1. The magnetic needle of a compass.

The aggregation of the earth's magnetic forces in the polar regions attracts and draws toward itself the magnetic force contained in the needle. The northern force is trying to draw the force out of the magnetic needle. The northern force is unable to do this because the elements composing the needle have a stronger power over the force. Although the polar force is inadequate to draw the force out of the needle, it has, however, the power to draw the super-magnetized point of the needle towards itself and hold it there. If the polar force could draw the force out of the needle, the needle would become inoperative, like a de-magnetized surface of the earth. If the sun like the polar magnetic force could not draw the forces out of the earth's crust, the earth, like the magnetic needle, would remain stationary. She would not revolve on her axis.

Example 2. A spool of cotton.

With a spool of cotton I shall show the principle on which the earth is revolved on her axis.

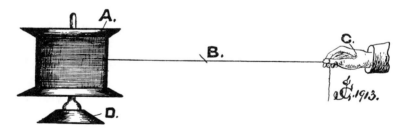

Revolving a spool of cotton. A. The spool of cotton on a spindle. B. The cotton being drawn off the spool. C. The force pulling the cotton. D. The spindle representing the earth's axis

The hand C will represent the sun's affinitive magnetic forces. B. The cotton—will be the earth's forces affinitive to the sun's.

When the hand pulls on the thread, the spool turns on the spindle—revolves. So when the earth's forces are being unwound (drawn out), they, like the thread, revolve the earth (the spool). Both the earth and the spool revolve on account of resistance.

Should the thread be loose on the spool, the thread only would revolve and not the spool. If there were no resistance to the sun's pull, the forces would leave the earth's crust without revolving her.

If there were no end to the thread, and the force pulling the thread was not of a temporary mechanical character, but an everlasting force, the spool, like the earth, would go on revolving to the end of time.

The Last Magnetic Cataclysm. Magnetic cataclysms have visited the earth at various times since she first commenced her existence. They are, however, unknown to our present-day scientists; although they were known, perfectly understood, and written about by our forefathers of the earth's first great civilization more than 25,000 years ago. All of our conglomerate rocks are the result of magnetic cataclysms, and were not formed by sedimentary deposits, as asserted by geology. The ancient knowledge about magnetic cataclysms was carried down to within 3500 years ago, as shown in Egyptian writings during the reign of Sti 2nd.

What Is a Magnetic Cataclysm? Before explaining what a magnetic cataclysm is, it will be well to point out that the earth has been subjected to two forms of cataclysms, arising from two distinct causes. First, the volcanic cataclysm arising from volcanic workings. These cataclysms affect local areas only. Second, the magnetic cataclysm, caused by a lurch of the earth going back into magnetic balance. This affects all the waters of the earth to a greater or less extent.

As previously stated, a magnetic cataclysm results from the earth getting out of magnetic balance. The earth is out of magnetic balance when her pole gets drawn towards the sun more than $23\frac{1}{2}°$ from its mean position. When the pole has been drawn more than $23\frac{1}{2}°$ from mean, the earth's gyroscopical force carries it back at too great a velocity, which causes a displacement of the earth's surface waters.

When the pole is carried back at too great a velocity, its impetus for a time overpowers the earth's cold magnetic force, so that the great central magnet is unable to hold the waters in their normal position. Consequently they get "spilled."

With the lurch of the earth, causing the pole's too rapid progress, waves are formed commencing at the poles, which run one north, the other south, on the two opposite sides of the earth. As these two polar waves leave the polar regions, the waters of the equatorial regions begin to flow towards the poles, on one side of the earth towards the south pole, and on the opposite side of the earth towards the north pole. These waves fill in the hollows in the polar regions, and once more level off the waters. It is thus seen that it is a movement of water completely around the earth, but unequal in height in various regions. The maximum displacement has always been in the polar regions, and the minimum displacement of the waters has always been in the equatorial regions.

During the early part of the earth's history, magnetic cataclysms were of frequent occurrence, as shown by various rock formations. They continued down to the end of the Tertiary Era, when the earth's crust had been so thickened and compacted that the earth went into the final magnetic balance.

As the earth's crust thickened and compacted, so the storage-house for her forces was increased in capacity. And magnetic cataclysms became less frequent as the volume of forces stored increased.

From the first magnetic cataclysm down to, but not including the last one, the waves consisted of water only. When the last one occurred, it was after vast fields of ice had been formed in the polar regions. When the lurch came and the waves started, all ice at the poles was broken loose and carried along by the waves. The equatorial waters carried no ice.

To establish a final condition, neutral zones had to be established between the forces; where cooling was concerned, the cessation of thickening and cooling brought about the final stationary condition.

A neutral zone between the forces, operating in the thickening and cooling of the earth's crust, appears at first glance to be in direct defiance of the law of equalization. As a matter of fact, however, it was principally the law of equalization which formed the neutral zone.

In using the word final magnetic balance, I wish to convey the fact that the earth had been in and out of magnetic balance many times before, and that the one in question was the last and the final one.

Now all the forces which could change or cause an irregularity in the movements of the poles have become equalized in power. Therefore the workings and movements of the poles from the time of the last balancing to the end of all time must be perfectly even and continuous without variation or irregularities as heretofore.

The final magnetic balancing of the earth was one of the greatest and most sublime of the supreme works of the Creator. Every point and detail was worked out beyond human con-

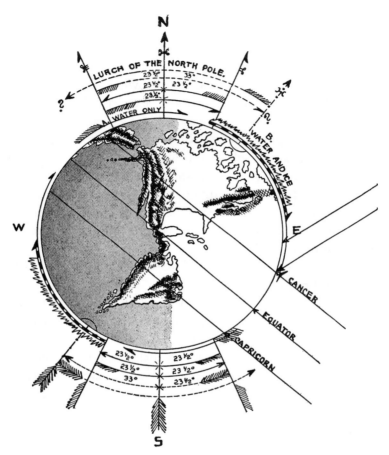

The pole's lurch

N. North pole at its mean position.   S. South pole at its mean position.   A. Normal western limit of the pole 23½° from mean.   B. Normal eastern limit of the pole 23½° from mean.   C. Point in east where pole was drawn before the lurch.   D. The path of the pole to this eastern point.   E. The path of the pole lurching to the west. F. The point west where the pole reached.   1 and 2. The normal variations from the equator.   3. The point reached with the sun vertical at D. X^1. Waves of water with mountains of ice rushing towards the south. X^2. Wave of water only rushing north. W^1. Waves of water with mountains of ice rushing towards the north. W^2. Wave of water only traveling southerly.

ception. Preparations for this step were commenced before the waters rested upon the hot scorching rocks which formed the earth's surface, and developments in the earth's crust were continuous from the Archaean time down to the day of accomplishment.

THE CATACLYSM. At the end of the Tertiary Era the earth's north pole had been drawn several degrees to the east of the point of safety which ended in a magnetic cataclysm.

This was the last of the magnetic cataclysms that was to visit the earth. It was the last one the earth will ever see, because with this cataclysm the earth went into:

Final Magnetic Balance.

By final I mean that the earth's crust having thickened and compacted sufficiently to hold a sufficient volume of her forces, it has become impossible again to upset her magnetic balance. By holding and retaining a sufficient volume of forces in her body, first, it prevents the sun's forces from pulling the pole beyond the point of safety; second, the sun's pull on the forces retained in the earth's body prevents the gyroscopical force from hurling the pole back. It is a checkrein.

One reason why a volume of the earth's forces is retained in her body is that the earth's atmosphere can only hold and carry in suspension a given volume of the earth's forces. After the sun's forces have drawn out all of the forces from the earth's body that the atmosphere can carry, there is still enough left in the earth's body to magnetize her surface, to act as a check against the gyroscopical force.

When all of the forces have been drawn out of the earth's body which the atmosphere can carry, the sun's forces can draw out no more until the exhausted forces return to earth for re-generation. Then the sun's pull, although existent, becomes so weakened as to enable the gyroscopical force to get control of the pole. This pull of the sun is what governs the rapidity at which the pole is carried back.

The earth's magnetic balance depends on the permanent volume of the earth's forces which are held in her body.

The earth's crust is the storehouse of her forces.

It may be as well at this point to say that the forces heretofore referred to are those contained in the first grand division of the earth's primary force and which I have called the electro-magnetic division. The sun has no power or influence over the second grand division—the cold-magnetic. This division holds all elements down and prevents movable matter from flying off into space.

The earth's forces are generated and re-generated along the great frictional line—the line of contact between the earth's hard crust and the molten matter in her center, and, as they are generated or re-generated, they are passed out into the storehouse, the hard crust, to be drawn upon as required by nature.

The sun is emitting excessively strong, governing, magnetic forces which are extremely affinitive to the forces in the first grand division of the earth's primary force, such as are super-magnetizing the polar regions.

Thus there are magnetic forces coming from the sun which are extremely affinitive to certain earthly forces, which is all that is necessary to show the cause of the last great magnetic cataclysm. The sun's magnetic forces, being so much more powerful than the magnetic pull of the great central magnet, draw from the earth's body out into her atmosphere as much as the atmosphere can carry.

At the end of the Tertiary Era the capacity of the earth's storehouse for her forces, due to the thickening and compacting of her crust, was not only adequate to supply the call from the sun but to retain a surplus of forces in the storehouse, after the earth was in balance. But when this condition had arrived, the earth's pole had in the meantime been drawn forward many degrees beyond the point of safety, and had to be returned to mean before a perfect balance could be established.

From the Archaean Time down to the end of the Tertiary Era, the resistance of the earth's central magnet was insufficient to prevent the sun's affinitive forces from drawing so much of the earth's forces out of her body in the polar regions during the long continued presence of the sun in this area that the volume left in the earth's body was totally inadequate to form the necessary check against the power of the gyroscopical force, which resulted in the sun's pulling the pole far beyond the point of safety, as shown in Arrow C in the diagram on page 212.

With the earth's polar surface virtually de-magnetized, the sun's pull was virtually eliminated. The control of the earth was now surrendered by the sun to the gyroscopical force. This force then proceeded to carry the pole back to its mean position—true north. Thus to set the earth in her upright position again.

After the pole was once started on her backward course, without any check or drag from the sun, it gradually increased in velocity until:

It became a perfect lurch.

When the last magnetic cataclysm occurred, all of the ice in the polar regions was loosened and broken up by the lurch, and the waters spilled. Huge waves of water were formed carrying mountains of ice on their crests, ice that had been forming for thousands of years. This great cataclysm of ice and water rolled down over about one-half of the northern hemisphere. Another great wave of water only rolled up towards the pole from the equatorial regions on the opposite side.

The last magnetic cataclysm, without doubt, caused greater loss of life and destruction to property than any magnetic cataclysm that preceded it, for, in addition to the water of the preceding ones, this one had mountains of ice accompanying it. This great wave of water and ice swept down to about the 40° parallel north latitude in North America and to about the 50° in Europe. Geologically, these boundaries show where the ice stopped and formed the "drift line." The waters, however, as is geologically and traditionally shown, extended much further. These waters flooded the lands and wiped out all life. Among other traditions, a Pueblo Indian tradition states that the waters reached as far south as New Mexico.

The mountains of ice and water rolling, tumbling, and grinding, wiped out all forms of life and turned them into pulp, so that now, within the regions over which the ice swept, there remains but a few fragments to tell us that life ever existed in these regions. A few parts of skeletons of man and his artifacts, such as arrow and spearheads, have been found in the gravel beds formed by the dying waters, and the works of man have been found in Nebraska, where Professor Gilder found their homes at the end of tunnels underneath the ground. These people, as is shown by their artifacts, had attained a high civilization. The waters and ice swept over the plains above their homes; the drift filled up the tunnels leading to their houses, and thus for a time sealed up the evidences of their existence.

While the water and ice were sweeping down over one-half of the northern hemisphere in a southerly direction, huge cataclysmic waves of water without ice were sweeping up in a northerly direction over the opposite half of the northern hemisphere.

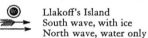
Llakoff's Island
South wave, with ice
North wave, water only
Showing where the great cataclysmic waves inundated
the eastern Asiatic plains

These great cataclysmic waves rolled up over the plains of Manchuria, Mongolia, and Siberia, the northeastern part of Asia, and ended in the Arctic Ocean.

As the waters swept up over these great Eastern Asiatic plains, they gathered up in their deathly embrace untold numbers of the mighty Siberian mammoths and other animals whose domicile was on the plains. Their bodies were carried along in the rushing waters and finally deposited in bulk in the Arctic Ocean, just off the mouth of the river Lena. Their bones and tusks now form an island called Llakoff's Island. As many of the skeletons are found virtually intact, it is proof positive that no ice accompanied this wave. Otherwise they would have been ground to pieces, as they were on the opposite side of the hemisphere. Confirming this, there are no ice marks anywhere in Northern Asia, but incontrovertible geological evidences of a north-running wave of water especially along the Valley of the river Lena.

The scene of the last great magnetic cataclysm is vividly pictured on my mind. I have attempted a sketch of it, but my brush has failed to convey fully my mind's impression. I have failed to bring out the details of the horrors and frenzies of the animal life. My sketch depicts the huge mountains of ice and water as they swept down over the plains of North America, roaring! pounding! grinding! and crunching! On, on, it comes, ever nearer and nearer, with ever-increasing roar and din. The earth quivers and shakes as the mighty forces assault her. The sun from mid-heavens races to the horizon and then disappears, leaving black darkness to enhance the terrors, then lightning shafts begin to fill the black heavens.

My mind pictures the panic-stricken and terrified forest animals, rushing aimlessly hither and thither in their frenzied terror, not knowing which way to turn or go to get away from the oncoming doom.

Herds of ponderous mastodons ran first one way, then another, screaming and trumpeting, with the horse shrieking in unison with the terrified howls of other animals, but all in vain. The jaws of death closed o'er them, they were all ground to a pulp and completely obliterated, man included.

With irresistible fury and force the mountains of ice and water crushed and ground to a pulp all that lay in their paths. For over a thousand miles this great wave extended back. A mountain of ice falls from the crest of the waters upon an exposed rock surface, the jagged ridge of an old archaean gas chamber; the rocks are splintered and broken by the impact. With contemptuous fury, the wave gathers up the splintered parts, then rolls and tumbles them along for hundreds of miles, as if they were mere pebbles or grains of sand. This

[218]

THE NORTH WAVE OF THE LAST MAGNETIC CATACLYSM. NO ICE ACCOMPANIED IT
SEE ITS RESULTS IN EASTERN ASIA AND WESTERN ALASKA, N.A.

THE SOUTH RUNNING WAVE OF THE LAST MAGNETIC CATACLYSM, THE
BIBLICAL FLOOD, AND THE GEOLOGICAL MYTH — THE GLACIAL PERIOD

[221]

rude tumbling of the splintered rocks made boulders out of them, some of which were hundreds of tons in weight. Eventually the wave began to die down, and, as it died down, eddies were formed in various places. Here the drift began to settle. When the waters had completely passed on, then the ice in these settlements melted and the rock sand and gravel settled and became unstratified drift, which we find in many spots where the ice cataclysm passed over.

As the wave was dying down, huge rushing currents of mixed matter, water, ice, gravel, sand, and small boulders were formed. As these currents began to weaken, they began to drop their loads. The first to settle were the heaviest, and then gradually down to the finest, so that along these courses we now find a stratified deposit. Today we find our river and valley drift stratified. Along these courses the flowing ice and drift scratched and planed the stationary rocks,—scratchings and planings which are in evidence to this day. Along the plains at many points the eddies left their deposits. Subsequently the mountains were raised along these plains; as the land was lifted up, the drift went with it, so that now on the tops of some of our mountains we find boulders that have the markings made on them by the ice.

Let us look at the land after all the ice was melted and the waters had found their level.

What a land!! desolation everywhere, a desert of mud! mud! mud! as far as vision could reach and for thousands of miles beyond, with here and there hillocks and stretches of sand and gravel. In paths boulders raised their heads out of the mud, marking the lines of greatest destruction. Here and there are to be seen groups of huge boulders of hundreds of tons each, grim and silent monuments telling the tale to coming man, as one succeeded the other, of this terrible tragedy of the past.

Where are the forests primeval that adorned this land but a few days ago? Where are the great herds of mastodons who roamed and grazed throughout the land? And where is man that dominated all? Gone! all gone! They have all been crushed and ground into a pulp and mixed with the mud as a fertilizer. Never since the beginning of life upon earth has the soil received such a digging over and fertilizing, nor has she ever received such a cultivating since.

Our orchard trees with branches breaking down with fruit, our profusion of vegetables, our galaxy of flowers, and our fields of golden grain, were only made possible by this great preparation of the earth's surface—a kindly provision made by nature for the benefit of future man.

The last magnetic cataclysm was the great coping stone placed upon the house prepared for man by the great Creator.

From the foregoing it will be seen that I do not accept the geological theory of a glacial period, a theory in opposition to all natural laws. I have shown what the phenomenon was, which sustains my argument.

The last magnetic cataclysm is the same as the Biblical "flood."

Addenda

GEOLOGY AND THE COSMIC FORCES. The Birth of the Earth. I will commence this chapter by copying what is said about the creation, in the sacred writings of Mu. There the creation has been divided into seven commands of the Creator. It was written over 70,000 years ago in Mu.

Extracts: "The first intellectual command was: 'Let the gases which are scattered throughout space be collected together, and with them let worlds be formed.' Then the gases were brought together into whirling circulating masses."

"The second intellectual command was 'Let these gases cool and solidify.' Obeying this command, some of the gases cooled, solidified and formed round worlds. Gases were left on the outside of these worlds and there were gases contained within them. Darkness prevailed and there was neither light or sound, for as yet the atmosphere had not been created."

"The third intellectual command was: 'Let the outside gases be separated, so that they form the atmosphere and the waters.' Then the outside gases were divided; one part went to form the waters, and the remainder formed the atmosphere. The light and heat were contained in the atmosphere.

"The waters settled upon the face of the earth and covered it so that no dry land appeared above the waters anywhere.

"Then the shafts of the sun struck the light which was in the atmosphere and gave it life, and light shone upon the face of the earth, and the shafts of the sun struck the heat in the atmosphere, and also gave it life, so that warmth fell upon the face of the earth."

[225]

"The fourth intellectual command was: 'Let the land appear above the waters.' Then the gaseous fires of the underneath, which were contained within the earth, lifted the land upon which the waters rested, and the land appeared above the face of the waters."

Commands 5, 6 and 7 refer to life only.

After a careful study of these old Naacal writings, I made a study of the chemistry of the earth's crust, rock formations, and geological phenomena, to ascertain how well it fitted in with the writings of the earth's first great civilization.

It is left with my readers to say whether or not our present day scientists appear as mere babes in swaddling clothes compared with our great scientific forefathers.

It may be thought that Cosmic Forces have nothing to do with geology; directly they do not, but indirectly they control everything. The Cosmic Forces, as has been shown, are responsible for the earth's spin, and the earth's spin has been, and is, responsible for all volcanic workings.

To perfectly comprehend the workings of the great forces which eventually brought the earth into final magnetic balance I think it well to first give a short synopsis of the birth of the earth. Geologists have built up their theories on elements and compounds of elements coming before them.

I shall take the same material, and also show what part the Cosmic Forces and thermo-chemistry played.

After considering many of the questionable phenomena, I think the geologists' deductions about them are erroneous; and that these errors have arisen from the fact that geologists, generally, have completely ignored the presence of the great forces; also, the peculiar honeycombed condition of the earth's foundational structure, the primary archaean rock-granite. This honeycombed condition must necessarily have existed;

the reasons why will be given hereafter.

One of the greatest errors made by geologists is the manner in which molten matter cools and solidifies.

The process of cooling molten matter to the point where it becomes a solid is: first, a thin shell of crystals is formed on the outside of the mass, thus forming a crust or wall. When this crust or wall is formed there is no material shrinkage in the size of the body until the time when the whole mass solidifies, and is brought down to atmospheric temperature. Therefore, the earth's crust, when passing from a molten into a solid state, did not materially shrink. The only shrinkage in the size of a body is the reduction in the size or contraction of the crystals, which form the outside wall or skin, when they are brought down to atmospheric temperature. Thus, taking a spherical body, the only shrinking in the diameter of the body would be the amount of contraction of two crystals, one on each side of the sphere, which is infinitesimal. So that when the earth cooled, she never lost any size through cooling.

I can imagine how this assertion will be met by geologists, scientists and unthinking laymen. With flushed faces, sneers and loud speaking they will declare: "Why, it has been positively proven that the diameter of the earth has shrunk 20 miles in cooling." I am not going to argue with them that the earth since the beginning has not lost 20 miles of her diameter, because I thoroughly agree with them in the amount of shrinkage; but as to whether the shrinkage was due to contraction in cooling, I emphatically say it was not. Further, had the contraction been due to cooling, the great divine laws of creation as laid down by the Creator could not have been carried out.

I will explain how the crust of the earth was cooled and

solidified, following a natural law, which we see exemplified every day. I speak from practical experience in cooling and solidifying large masses of molten matter.

As soon as the outside wall or crust is formed, by a skin of outside molten matter cooling and turning into crystals, and joining each other, the molten matter within the crust follows; it gradually cools and forms crystals; and, as each new crystal forms, it attaches itself to the one previously formed, which lies on the outside. Thus it goes on until the whole mass is crystallized and the mass which was molten becomes a solid.

As will be seen, the building up of the solid has taken place from the outside and was continued inwards to the center.

When molten matter cools and crystallizes, each portion of molten matter that goes to form a crystal occupies more space than the crystal itself; consequently, as the building goes on, the adhesions of the planes of the crystal become reduced in area, thereby reducing the strength of the whole, and the strength of the adhesion between crystals.

A careful survey of the foregoing shows that as the building goes on, the proportion of molten matter in each crystal diminishes, although the size generally remains the same; hence there is a weakness. The outside crust never sinks in towards the center to meet the strains put upon the central crystals.

This condition with the further cooling of the mass brings about internal strains within the body, which are gradually intensified as the temperature of the mass drops down to atmospheric temperature. This is caused by the withdrawal of the heat force from the mass. I have previously shown that heat is a force occupying space, and that temperature is the measurement of the volume of heat present.

It can now be readily appreciated that when the heat is

withdrawn from super-heated body, cooling from a molten state, the central crystals of the mass, instead of having the bolstering power of a force, replaces it with a vacuum, so that the adhesions become weakened, often resulting in actually breaking the adhesions, causing long cracks to be formed in the body of the mass. Quite often when casting steel ingots, a regular hollow is formed in the ingot if the metal is poured too hot. This is technically called "piping." This condition only occurs when cooling metal from a molten state, and occurs because in building up to the outside crust all material has been drawn from the center, leaving it hollow. The outside crust does not contract to fill in the cracks or pipe in the ingot. Neither has the earth's crust shrunk to fill in the cracks and fissures in the primary rock which were formed there during the cooling of it. These cracks and fissures in the earth's foundational rocks were formed there for nature's purposes. They were pre-ordained to carry out creation as planned by the Creator. This will hereafter be shown and explained.

The formation of the primary rock, granite, was an undeveloped foundation which required compacting before a heavy super-structure could be built upon it. The development and completing of this foundation was the reason for most of the changes that took place in the earth's surface during the past millions of years. It was the cause of the many submersions and emersions of lands that have taken place during the many millions of years which elapsed between the archaean time, and the end of the tertiary era. Gases have been the active forces which have been the agents of these changes. Gases are responsible for our mountains and mountain ranges. They have been responsible for the depths of our oceans and seas; and gases are responsible for our earthquakes and volcanoes today.

Had the gases remained inactive from the beginning, not one inch of land would ever have appeared above the waters.

The gases were encased in and within the primary archaean rock for a purpose: to become the agents for bringing the land above the waters, digging it over, forming soil on it, cultivating it, and preparing it for the advent of man. Man could not appear before the proper condition for his existence had been completed; when this condition was completed man appeared.

GASES. First Command. I shall make a start with the earth's original form which was gaseous. I make the start from this point because it will better enable my readers to follow my ideas and conceptions concerning the disposition of various gases during the earth's cooling, the gases which went to form the earth's nebula.

Gases have been responsible for all of the most important changes that have taken place in the earth's topography from time to time. The workings of the gases account for many well-known phenomena, the origin of which are, and always have been, matters of mystery and controversy among scientists.

The earth's nebula was a whirling, circulating mass of hot elementary gases, which has been estimated to have been from 400,000 to 450,000 miles in diameter. Before proceeding further let us make sure that the earth's original form was gaseous, as stated in the sacred inspired writings of Mu.

To arrive at the original and primary state of any elementary body, we have to invoke the aid and assistance of chemistry. A chemical analysis is the undoing of a previous chemical action called a synthesis. A chemical analysis is therefore the untying of a previously made chemical knot. The last chemical analysis or the untying of the last chemical knot must therefore bring matter back to its original form.

A chemical analysis brought about by the aid of the common acids does not bring the matter back to original form; it only separates the elements of a compound, and then not perfectly, as there is still left what are termed impurities. I must therefore employ a higher branch of the science for further progress in the analysis. I will therefore employ thermo-chemistry, where the final analysis is brought about by the aid of the force heat, which transforms the elements into gases.

As there is no known form of analysis beyond this, we may presume that we have arrived at original form. This confirms the sacred writings and proves that what is now the solid crust of the earth was originally elementary gases.

As a further proof that the foregoing is correct, with the aid of heat turn earthly elements into gases; then, in turn cool the gases again. They return to solids, thus proving beyond question that the original form of the earth was gaseous. As an example of this nature today, let me call attention to what has been termed dust clouds which commonly appear after a major volcanic eruption. This is a well-known phenomenon to scientists. After a major eruption vast dust clouds are to be seen at high altitudes in the atmosphere, so dense as to often affect the sunlight. These clouds have been reported to extend thousands of miles, half way around the earth.

The ejections from the volcanoes normally are lava, which is molten rock, flames and smoke. It is inconceivable that the super-heated flames could carry up fine particles of dust without melting them and turning them into gases. The heat in the belt has been at a temperature sufficiently high to melt the rocks and form lava out of them; the dust was also in the belt, why was it not melted with the rocks? To me this is the only reasonable solution of these clouds: The dust left the crater in the form of super-heated gases, and being hot ascended; the higher they were carried, the cooler became the temperature; the flames were made up of both non-solidifying and solidifying gases. When the solidifying gases arrived at the cold strata of the earth's upper atmosphere, it caused them to cool and solidify in the form of a fine dust, making what science has called dust clouds.

These dust clouds float on until drawn down to the surface of the earth, by the great central magnet. After settling on the land, the first rain would naturally carry it into the soil, and where it fell on water it would naturally sink to the bottom.

In this way we see nature taking from the center to add to the surface. No doubt electric storms have much to do with bringing the dust down to the surface from the atmosphere.

Cooling the Gases of the Earth's Nebula. The great universal centripital force, if it can be so called, gathered up the earth's gases out in space, and worked them to a center.

We see this same thing happening today in various spots of the universe. One which I think duplicates the earth's nebula, moon and all, appears in the constellation of Andromeda.

When the gases were brought to a center by the great molding force, they had an exceedingly high temperature, which is demonstrated by the fact that now to turn the matter back into original form, an exceedingly high temperature is required.

Whether it was the effect of ether surrounding the cooling gases, whether it was the dividing of the gases themselves, or chemical affinities, or the great molding force, or a combination of them all, I am not prepared to say; but, certain of the various gases went into chemical compounds and intimate unions, cooled, solidified and formed the initial crust of the earth.

There were more than 80 elementary gases composing the earth's nebula. Out of this number only six went to form the initial rock granite, namely — aluminum, calcium, magnesium, potassium, silicon and oxygen. Hereafter I will call these six the solidifying gases and the balance non-solidifying.

At the time when some of the gases began to assume a molten form, they apparently began to divide to a certain extent only; apparently right in the middle of the nebula an area of the heavy rock-making gases was drawn towards the center in the form of a sphere. With it however were carried vast volumes of the non-solidifying variety. A complete separation between the solidifying and non-solidifying gases was not made, so the earth's crust commenced to be formed with the gases unseparated.

As previously stated the cooling and solidifying commenced near the center of the nebula. Volumes of gases of all sorts lay within the forming crust and volumes of gases of all sorts lay on the outside of the crust. Among the outside gases were vast volumes of the heavy, solidifying gases. These gases eventually went to form the gneiss rocks, which were laid down upon the granite. The balance of the outside gases went to form the atmosphere and waters. The material of the gneiss rocks went into various chemical combinations and, one after the other, cooled until molten, then rested on the gneiss. The earth was moving at the time and her impetus caused the molten matter to spread and flow. As these rocks were not all formed at the same time, but one after the other, they were stratified. This is the reason why we find the gneiss rocks stratified and the granite unstratified, although some of the earliest of the gneiss rocks are made of identically the same chemical compound as the granite.

The granite at the time the first gneiss rocks were being laid down was exceedingly hot. It had not sufficiently solidified to prevent the gneiss from running into it.

During the formation of the granite rock, some of the non-solidifying gases went into chemical combination with each other, forming highly explosive gases, which are now called volcanic gases.

These volcanic gases were encased in and within the granite rock. In the granite rock they formed chambers for themselves, and vast volumes were incased within the crust itself. These confined gases could not escape without first puncturing the rock above. This they were incapable of doing at first, because the rocks were too hot and too pliable.

As the granite rock was being formed by one set of gases, at the same time the explosive volcanic gases were being formed by another set of gases, so that in and within the granite rock there were huge volumes of these explosive gases awaiting freedom.

How the Explosive Gases Formed Chambers for Themselves. As vast volumes of the volcanic gases were associated with the solidifying gases at the time the granite rock was being formed, room space was required for their accommodation. These gases could not remain evenly distributed throughout the solidifying mass, as in such a state they would have prevented the formation of rock by preventing the adhesion of the crystals as they were formed. Had this adhesion of crystals been prevented, only hot masses of powderlike, crumbly matter could have been formed.

These volcanic gases collected in bulk, forming huge bubbles; the rock was formed around them, and thus incased them. In this way a huge chamber was formed in the granite rock, filled with the most explosive form of gases.

From the foregoing it will be seen that granite, the foundation of the earth when laid down, was a perfectly honeycombed mine of explosive gases. In an estimate I have made of the possible volume of these gases, I think fully one-half of the rock was made up of these chambers, and that up to the end of the Tertiary Era, by the blowing out of these chambers down to the gas belt line, fully 20 miles of the earth's diameter was reduced. I made this calculation on the average depth of the gas belts today. It was by the blowing out of these chambers, and their roofs falling to their floors, that the earth's diameter was reduced, and not by shrinkage in cooling. I think this should end the teaching of the geological myth of "the fault," upon which our scientists are basing the origin of earthquakes. The origin of an earthquake is the movement of gases, and gases only, attempting to reach one of the outlets in a belt, and, finding the passage blocked, they have to clear it to pass on.

When a chamber was blown out the roof fell to the floor, the waters rolled in over it, and then another super-structurical rock was formed upon it.

Regarding the size of these chambers, they no doubt varied considerably. Some were mere pockets a few feet in height only, while others were hundreds and thousands of miles long and of great height and area. The average was less than 300 feet in height from floor to roof. This is verified where we find a coral limestone built up on the roof of a fallen chamber.

I do not think that the deepest spots in our oceans are the result of the blowing out of a single chamber. I rather think that a series of chambers lay directly under one another, and close at that.

Following natural laws these old archaean gas chambers should represent area rather than height. This seems to be verified by several phenomena following a blowout.

All through the past millions upon millions of years, from the Archaean Time down to the end of the Tertiary Era, the earth's foundation rock, granite, has been sliced up through volcanic workings. The land and rocks have been raised and submerged over and over again. Each time they have been compacted by the weight of water above, so that now nearly all if not entirely all of the old archaean gas chambers, anywhere near the surface of the earth, have been blown out, worked over and compacted. If any do remain they are exceedingly small, mere pockets, and of the isolated variety; that is, they have no connection with the earth's center or cracks and fissures leading to the earth's center. At present for many miles below the earth's surface (down to the gas belt lines) the primary rock is a solid foundation for the superstructure resting upon it.

ELIMINATING CHAMBERS. I have already shown that the earth's crust was full of cracks and fissures caused by internal strains in cooling; these became the passageways for the gases from the earth's center to the chambers above.

The earth's center is composed of all of the elementary gases which formed the nebula. They are the gases "within." Much of the heavy gases has gone into a molten state, leaving the non-solidifying gases free. The earth revolving on her axis is carrying around this molten matter, but not at so rapid a gait as the crust is moving. This causes a friction between the central molten matter and the hard crust. This frictional line forms a magnet, and is the source of what is termed gravity.

[236]

It has two divisions, as heretofore explained. The friction is enhanced by the central centrifugal force thrusting it against the hard crust.

As they are being carried around, the free gases come into contact with the hard crust. By the tremendous weight of the molten matter driven against the crust by the unmeasurable power of the central centrifugal force, the free gases are forced up into the cracks and crevices to the chambers. They are forced from the lowest down chamber to the one nearest the surface. This one, being already full, has to find room space for the new gases thrust upon it. This it does by raising the roof of the chamber, this being the line of least resistance. As new gases flow or are driven in, so the roof is forced up. This goes on until the thickness of the roof will stand no more raising. Weak spots in it have developed; these the gases puncture, and escape as volcanoes. When they have been exhausted down to the point where their bolstering power ceases to sustain the weight of the roof, the roof crashes down. The fallen rocks seal up the passage to the chamber below. Then the chamber below has to take charge of the new gases from the earth's center. This it does until it meets the fate of the one just blown out above it, and so it has gone on until the accumulated rocks above are thicker than the gases can lift and puncture. They then attempt to lift and puncture the rocks above. This they are incapable of doing. The rocks are lifted until a huge tunnel is formed to the next lateral chamber, and so on from one chamber to another, thus forming a belt. At spots the gases found weak spots in the roof; these they followed up, eventually piercing the roof and forming a crater through which the gases of the belt are emptied out. In places the forming of these belts cracked the roof above so that the gases had a free passage to an isolated chamber which was upholding land out of water. This they caused to be overcompressed. It then blew out and the land above with all on it sank and became submerged. Prominent instances of this in the past are the submersion of Mu, Atlantis, Bering Land Bridge, overland route to Europe and ancient Ceylon. At places there were no chambers to run into; the belt then bored along in the lines of least resistance, raising mountains and mountain ranges.

These gas belts could not form until after the rock above was too thick to raise and puncture. This occurred about 12,500 to 13,000 years ago, so that mountains, as I have always maintained, are of comparatively recent origin.

When the gas belts were being formed, vast areas of land were submerged and water was drawn in from surrounding areas to fill in the holes made by these submergences. This emerged much land that was covered by shallow water, and extended the shore lines of remaining lands, also draining out shallow arms of seas which ran up into the land. Notable examples of this are the draining out of the Amazon sea in South America, the Mississippi valley sea and the St. Lawrence valley sea in North America, the emersion of Florida and extension of the shore lines of America, both on the east and the west sides.

The body of the earth today is honeycombed with gas belts large and small. There are two particularly large ones. One is the Great Central Belt, which runs around the world in the northern equatorial regions; this belt has two divisions and many ramifications. The other is the Pacific Circuit Belt which runs clear around the Pacific; this has several divisions and many ramifications. The Pacific Circuit Belt has more volcanoes on it than all the rest of the world put together.

NATURAL LAWS. At the commencement of creation, universal laws were laid down for the completion of the earth's development. These laws have been unswervingly followed from the beginning down to the present time. They are commonly known as the natural laws. These laws have ever been governed and carried into effect by the forces.

Many of the natural laws are well understood to exist, but what controls them is not known. It will be my endeavor in this work to supply to science this missing link. It is not my intention to review all of the natural laws, but rather to call attention to a few that are the least understood and appreciated by laymen.

The natural laws to which I am about to call attention should be appreciated and understood, as they will enable the reader more thoroughly to understand what forces are and their manner of working, especially the workings of the earth's great primary force with its multiplicity of branches.

EXTREMES. By using the word "extreme" to designate this natural law, I wish to specialize it from any other of the natural laws.

An extreme is that which cannot be received by the human body, or comprehended by the human mind. Although extremes exist, they cannot be seen, felt or comprehended. There are also extremes which do not concern the body or the mind. All thoughtful and reasoning minds must appreciate that we are surrounded and living in the midst of tremendous, overpowering forces, many of which, if they could touch us, would instantly crush out our existence.

There is a great force which is carrying the earth around the sun, another which is daily spinning the earth on her axis, and yet another which is held in suspension in our atmosphere and which is capable of driving all the mechanical machinery of the world millions of times over, and yet another that if put into full force would burn everything that is combustible on the face of the earth, and fuse and melt the rocks and destroy the earth.

When man was created, he was formed tenderly, delicately and extremely complex; so fragile that if one of the great forces could touch him, he would be instantly crushed. Fortunately, however, these great forces cannot, generally, detrimentally touch him, or any element. Only one of these forces, and it is a secondary one, can affect elements, and this one comes from the earth herself.

No force emanating from the sun can touch or affect any earthly element.

Although being in the midst of and surrounded by the great forces, we cannot feel them, because they do not touch us; we cannot receive them because our elementary bodies are neutral to them.

Great, tremendous crushing forces are emanating from the earth herself. They are, however, so arranged in their workings that under all ordinary circumstances a sufficient volume is seldom accumulated at any one point that could harm us. Even then, when so accumulated, we must be in the direct line of their passage to receive them. As an example I shall take lightning, which is an accumulation of one of the divisions of the earth's primary force over and above what the atmosphere can hold in suspension.

A scale of reception has been created within us—that is, we are so constructed that we can only receive within certain ranges. These ranges are middle or medium. Beyond these ranges either high or low, they become extremes. Because they are extremes, we cannot receive them; therefore they cannot harm us. It matters not how powerful or how terrible the force may be, if it is beyond our range it cannot touch us. To this general rule I know of only one exception, and that is the case of lightning. I shall now give a few examples of extremes which are popularly known:

1. The human ear is limited in its range of reception. We can neither receive or hear a very high tone or a very low one.

2. The optic nerve is limited in its capacity for carrying the light force. It cannot carry to the brain a sufficient volume to injure the brain.

3. A quart of water cannot be put into a pint cup. When a pint of water is in the cup, the balance overflows. The balance is an extreme.

4. A bar of iron three inches in diameter cannot be passed through a hole two inches in diameter. The extra inch in the thickness of the bar is an extreme to the hole.

I shall now demonstrate the first two of these four examples.

Example 1—Sound. Let a number of people sit around a room, then in the center place one with a sliding whistle. Commence with its lowest note or tone, then gradually push in the slide and ascend the scale. At a certain high tone or note, one or more of the people in the room will cease to hear any sound coming from the instrument although the sound will be heard by every one else in the room. Continue raising the tone, then one after the other of the listeners will cease to hear any sound whatever from the whistle. Eventually no one will hear it. The foregoing shows that the range of reception of sound varies among people, some having a longer range than others.

As soon as the whistle is emitting a sound which no one can hear, bring into the room an ordinary domesticated cat. The cat on entering the room will at once prick up her ears and look at the whistle, for the cat hears a sound coming from the instrument. Pussy hears because her range of hearing reception is higher than that of human beings. The cat can be corroborated by a test of the sound waves coming from the whistle.

The foregoing demonstrates that there is an upper limit to the reception of sound by human beings; also that certain animals have a higher limit than human beings.

I shall now make a test for a low limit by selecting the lowest notes of a very large organ. Many people cannot hear them. Atmospheric sound waves and discernible vibrations confirm the fact that sound is there. This determines that there is also a low limit to the reception of sound by human beings, and that it also varies in different people. The ear, having both a high and low limit to the reception of sound, shows that man can only receive the middle or medium range. All sounds above the high limit and all sounds below the low limit are therefore extremes to the human being. Sounds, however, coming within the range of reception, may be so intensified as to become harmful to the hearing. Intensities of this description generally are the outcome of the works of man, and can therefore be guarded against by protection of the eardrum.

Example 2—The Optic Nerve. This is fully discussed in Chapter 3, entitled "Light," on pages 69 to 80.

The Mind.

The mind of man also is governed by extremes, for:

Man's mind cannot conceive where space begins or where it ends.

Man's mind cannot conceive when time began or when it will end.

These two questions are extremes to the human mind.

DUPLICATIONS. This is a great natural law but little understood or understood at all: the natural law of duplication.

The earth has been built up on a set of original patterns and laws. Each new life or whatever else it may be partook of the pattern of its predecessor. Changes to a slight degree took place in each succeeding pattern. This had to be to make them more complex to be balanced by the ever cooling of the earth, and the lowering of the volume of the life force proportionate to and in ratio with the temperature. The semi-duplication or semi-repetition of life has been erroneously called by scientists "evolution."

These semi-duplications in life had to be so to make them more complex, otherwise life would have died out with the first product. Then the earth today would only be a barren waste without life upon it. In this work, Chapter V, I show what life is and why each succeeding life was more complex than its predecessor, and why each succeeding life partook so strongly of the shape and character of its predecessor. I shall show that it was only following the great law of duplication.

A great field of duplications meets our eyes on all sides in the field of nature. A river starts with particles of moisture in the air. These particles of moisture form rain drops and fall, the rain drops soak into the ground and form springs, the springs join and form brooks, the brooks join and form streams, the streams form a river which flows majestically to the ocean. A tree starts from a seed.

A ray from a super-heated body starts as a dark invisible parent ray, then divides and sub-divides over and over again, ending in numberless colored rays. Each of these rays is carrying a force which is used by nature.

The earth's own great force starts as a parent primary force, then divides and sub-divides into innumerable forces, each particular force having its appointed work to do for nature.

The human nerve system and the human blood system are

other examples. And so I might go on indefinitely with examples of duplication.

THE SUPERIOR SUN. Our sun is revolving on her axis, therefore she is being governed by a superior sun, who also is revolving on her axis.

Astronomers have advanced the theory, and upon good sound reasoning, that, out in space, far beyond the great sun Rigel there is a great dark sun. The movements of celestial bodies and the appearance of an apparently unoccupied space in this part of the universe has led many scientists to this conclusion. Such a theory is well founded.

This great dark sun is believed to be many times larger than the largest of our known suns. No estimate, however, has been advanced regarding its possible size, nor could there be, when the body is dark and invisible.

Some foolish writers accepting the theory of a dark invisible sun go further and say that it is a dead sun. If it were a dead sun, it could be seen if within the range of our telescope, for reflected light would disclose its position and size. There are two good reasons why it may not be seen; first, it may be too far away to bring into view with our most powerful telescopes. But what is more probable is that her rays are dark and extremely intense, so intense that all are ultra to the human eye.

It seems a certainty that the superior sun around which our sun is revolving has never been seen, although possibly, but improbably, she may be nearer to us than suns which we do see. The superior sun is an incalculable distance beyond Rigel.

A sun powerful enough to control such an inconceivable space, with the tens of thousands of bodies under her control, must have rays and forces which are extreme to the human eye, and neutral to all earthly forces. As there is no unoccupied area of the universe except possibly by a dark invisible sun that lies out beyond Rigel, the possibility remains that every body we see in the heavens is under her control.

As the dark intense rays coming from our sun are ultra and extreme to the human eye, it stands to reason that the dark extremely intense rays coming from the superior sun are a thousand times more so. So, to man and to science, the supperior sun must always remain the dark secret.

THE END OF THE EARTH. The question "What will be the end of the earth?" has always been an interesting question and a speculation not only among scientists but among many laymen as well. The interest in the subject has brought many theories forward, and as I have shown, many of them ending in some calamity for this poor old earth.

I am going to add another one; as my readers will have seen ere now, it will not be scientifically orthodox.

The earth arrived at her final form and condition during the Pleistocene Period, which condition will last to the end of time.

Every body throughout the universe is moving in a neutral zone, and clear of all other bodies. To affect any of the celestial bodies, something must happen to the great supreme force which is controlling the universe. The neutral zones have been arranged so that no two bodies can collide or run into each other. Each sun controls its own satellites and has no power over others. No one system encroaches on or overlaps another. No body can be drawn from one system to another. The earth cannot become a dead world as long as our sun exists. Our temperatures and seasons cannot alter because the movements of the poles have been finally fixed.

Oxidations and erosions will continue. Mountains will gradually be washed down, and with the material carried down by the rivers into the seas, islands will be formed. Man will reclaim the land and make it more productive than when on the mountain side. Millions of years hence all of the volcanic gases will be worked out of the earth's body. Then earthquakes and volcanoes will belong to the past history of the earth.

Man will become better and more nearly perfect, living consistently with his great knowledge. Struggles and bickerings will be unknown. "The lion will lie down with the lamb." Nations with their cravings for power and wealth will disappear. There will be one great union of the communities of mankind, each one being in truth a brother to the other. Then:

The Supreme only knows what is to follow.

J. CHURCHWARD

1870–1934

This work was commenced in 1870 and has been revised, added to, and checked off five times between 1870 and 1934. It is now offered to the public.   J. C.

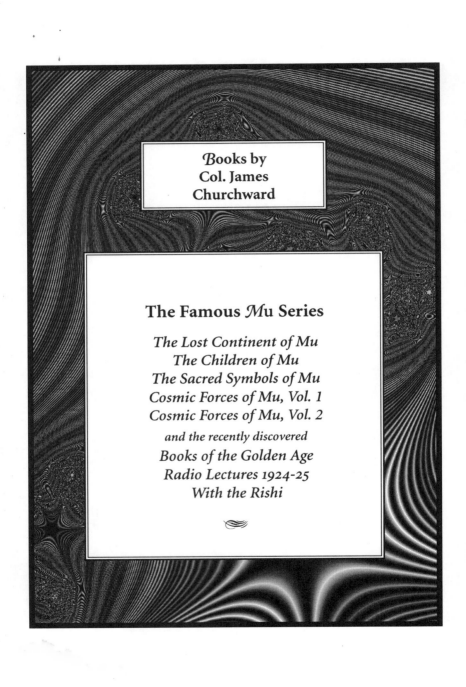

Books by
Col. James
Churchward

The Famous Mu Series

The Lost Continent of Mu
The Children of Mu
The Sacred Symbols of Mu
Cosmic Forces of Mu, Vol. 1
Cosmic Forces of Mu, Vol. 2
and the recently discovered
Books of the Golden Age
Radio Lectures 1924-25
With the Rishi